DOWN
FROM
TROY

Also by Richard Selzer:

Imagine a Woman and Other Tales
Taking the World in for Repairs
Letters to a Young Doctor
Confessions of a Knife
Mortal Lessons
Rituals of Surgery

DOWN FROM TROY

A

DOCTOR COMES OF AGE

RICHARD SELZER

LITTLE, BROWN AND COMPANY

BOSTON   NEW YORK   TORONTO   LONDON

First Paperback Edition

Published by arrangement with William Morrow and Company, Inc.

Parts of this book have appeared previously in a somewhat different form
in *The New York Times Magazine, Hartford Courant/Northeast Magazine, MD
Magazine, Missouri Review, Harper's Bazaar,* and *Hippocrates.*

Library of Congress Cataloging-in-Publication Data

Selzer, Richard.
  Down from Troy : a doctor comes of age / Richard Selzer. — 1st
  pbk. ed.
      p.   cm.
  Originally published: New York: W. Morrow, 1992.
  ISBN 0-316-78065-0
  1. Selzer, Richard, 1938- . 2. Physicians — New York — Biography.
I. Title.
R154.S358A3 1993b
610'.92 — dc20
  [B]   93-11302

10 9 8 7 6 5 4 3 2 1

RRD-VA

*Published simultaneously in Canada
by Little, Brown & Company (Canada) Limited*

Printed in the United States of America

For the grandchildren:
Becky
Hank
Emmy
Lucy
And for Bill Selzer

DOWN FROM TROY

Chapter 1

A childhood spent in the 1930s seems much more distant than sixty years, as though it had taken place a century before that, when the streets of Troy were gaslit. Between then and now, between Troy and New Haven, there is a chasm across which swings only the frayed rope bridge of memory. Besides, like any memoir of growing up, this one is an impersonation. The author, seeking to reenact his boyhood, cannot entirely shuck his manhood. The past remains beyond total recall, no matter the exactitude of the writer. If the telling seems to have a certain staccato rhythm, it is because the past remembered is made up of small, random bursts of turbulence and long periods of stagnation. More than once, I have tied dried apricots and paper leaves to the branches of a long-dead tree to give it the appearance of life. Oh, had I the muse for it, I would do as Homer did: wear vine leaves in my hair, strike a lyre with the flat of my hand and sing of Troy—tales of heroism, treachery, vengeance, single combat. Instead, I have only these unbaptized scraps to offer in the hope that, taken together, they will provide a glimpse of that time, that place. Perhaps they will also reveal how one boy grew up to become a doctor who writes. To Troy, then. Troy! Where in October even the dogs in the street pause to admire the foliage. Troy! Unfurling down the hillsides like the grayish pink tongue of a spaniel to lap the waters of the Hudson River.

Father was a general practitioner, one of a dozen or so who presided over the physical breakdown of the Trojans exacerbated by the poverty of the Great Depression. In addition to the usual degenerative diseases, there were rampant alcoholism, venereal infections and malnutrition. Birth defects were common and tuberculosis endemic. The phlegm on the cobblestones was apt to be red. In those days, general practitioners set broken bones, delivered babies and performed surgery. Surgery was Father's favorite. It was the "handsomeness" of the craft that he loved. I think now that the ritual and regalia of the operating room satisfied the hunger for religious faith that his natural skepticism denied him. It was from Father that I inherited a passionate interest in craft. The sight of skill and expertise in application is irresistible to me.

Once, Troy had had its day of grandeur. No house but peered out through an ophthalmic bay window at the second story; no stoop but wore a skirt of ornamental wrought iron. And so many churches as to make a stranger at the gates think himself about to enter the New Jerusalem. It gave the landscape the effect of wallpaper in which the pattern is repeated all around a room.

I lived in two houses in Troy. The first, on Second Street, was a three-story red-brick building with a high stoop and one of those curved wrought-iron railings. When I was seven years old, a fire caused us to move to an old brownstone on Fifth Avenue. In each house we lived right above Father's office. From my earliest days I sat on the landing and listened to the moans and cries that floated up the staircase. No words, only the howled vowels that were the language of pain, the inarticulate sounds of weeping that rose and fell above the steady rumble of Father's voice.

In the front windows of the first floor were plates of milk glass announcing the office hours: 1:00–3:00 P.M., 6:00–8:00 P.M.—which was absurd because Father would have been happy to see anybody at any time. During Father's office hours, my brother Billy and I were forbidden to speak out loud lest we disturb the sacred rites that were going on downstairs. I still have a little difficulty speaking out loud during those periods of time.

After eight o'clock, when Father came up for his dinner, Billy and I would sneak downstairs to the darkened consultation room and go to the glass front cabinet where he kept his medical textbooks. There, by the shamefaced light of a candle stub, we would look at pictures and spell out the words. Our favorite was the *Textbook of Obstetrics and Gynecology*. It was then and there that I first became aware of the rich, alliterative language of medicine. I remember that some of the best words began with the letter *C*. "Cerebellum," I said out loud and let the word drip off the end of my tongue like melted chocolate. "Carcinoma"—it sounded rather like that aria from *Rigoletto* that Mother used to sing. And then I learned the word that made a surgeon of me—"Choledochojejunostomy." All those syllables marching across the page, ending in that terminal *y*. It didn't matter what it meant—if that was the way surgeons talked, I was going to be one of them.

It was on one such nocturnal visit, when Billy was ten and a half and I nine, that Billy found a book on the bottom shelf all the way at the back and lying facedown so as to conceal its title. Lifted from the obscurity in which it had lain for heaven knows how long, it revealed itself to be an illustrated copy of *One Hundred Twenty Days of Sodom* by the Marquis de Sade. The cover was done in pale green silk with embossed gold lettering. The feel of it in my hands remains one of the two or three most exotic experiences of my life. O madly beat the hearts of Troy on that night of wild discovery! Of the illustrations I remember only that they were tumefacient. As for the prose, the best parts were walled up in Latin. Imagine the iron gate of Latin slammed in the face of puberty and you can imagine our suffering. It says something about Billy and me that in high school he studied math and physics while I took four years of Latin. By the time I had got to the orations of Cicero, I was able, barely, to translate the best parts of *One Hundred Twenty Days of Sodom*. I read it off to Billy, who was then in his senior year.

"Big deal," he said with studied nonchalance. But I was more profoundly impressed. Not so much with the behavior of the Sodomites as with the fact that Father had read it too. What could that mean? By then, he had been dead for two years. The very next day I sat in front of the coal stove and reenacted the biblical fate of Sodom page by page. Now, at last, Father could rest easy. He wouldn't be found out. It was my finest hour.

While my father embodied the world of science, my mother represented to me the world of art. She was a singer, possessed of a small pure soprano that sounded as though a white mouse were ringing a tiny silver bell. Troy had its share of bards and troubadours, but Mother was its only *artiste*. A woman given to wearing scarves of crushed silk, floating stoles and floppy hats, she used old-fashioned hairpins, the kind that were always falling out of the masses of her dark, polished hair. Throughout the Depression she never stopped singing, both at home and in amateur productions on the stage of the Troy Music Hall. After supper, doing the dishes in the kitchen, she would usually sing. When she didn't, I'd put down my book, go to the dish rack and start drying. Before you knew it, there would be "Caro nome" or "Ouvre ton coeur." Then came the long evening over a book, and the ticking of Grandpa's clock which had to clear its throat before striking the hour.

A hundred times a day, Mother sang. Sometimes no more than a brief burst of melody that blossomed without rhyme or reason in the vacancy of her mind, composed on the spot and vented as if to relieve the pressure of an excess of music.

Every June, the same catbird set up its nest in a lilac bush in the backyard. All summer it imitated her vocalizing, up and down the scale. One year she sang "Parigi o cara" from the last act of *Traviata* over and over again until the bird had it down pat and joined her in a duet. Needless to say, this caused a sensation among her next of kin and confirmed our suspicions that she was a witch. Draped about the voice was the ample figure and flamboyant personality of a diva. On the stage of the music hall, in a flowing tunic, with her arms thrown out like wings and an expression of such transport as to suggest headlessness, she looked for all the world like someone who had just flown in from Samothrace. Billy said she looked more like washing blown out on a clothesline. Indeed, she was the most expressive singer in the world, throwing bosom, eyebrows, earlobes and elbows into it. Once she sang "Ah, Sweet Mystery of Life" lying supine on the floor. Eyes either awash or ablaze, she ranged over the English music-hall repertoire, French art songs, lullabies and grand opera. A typical musical soiree in the parlor—at which attendance was strongly suggested—might include a pair of Civil War songs of the bathetic genre, which, by the sheer force of her personality, she transformed into touching lament.

From "Just Before the Battle, Mother":

> Farewell, Mother, you may never
> press me to your heart again
> But oh, you'll not forget me, Mother,
> if I'm numbered with the slain.

And its sequel, "Just After the Battle, Mother":

> Mother, dear, your Boy is wounded
> and the night is drear with pain
> But still I feel that I shall see you
> and the dear old home again.

These were followed by "Driven from Home":

> Out in this cold world, out in the street,
> Asking a penny of each one I meet
> Shoeless I wander about thro' the day
> Wearing my young life in sorrow away

and the equally fraught "Take Back the Heart That Thou Gavest":

> Take back the heart that thou gavest
> What is my anguish to thee?
> Take back the freedom thou cravest
> Leaving the fetters to me.

Her masterpiece was a duet between a brother and sister, Paul and Florence, in which she sang both parts. It was a lugubrious meditation on the roaring of the sea entitled "What Are the Wild Waves Saying?"

> FLORENCE [piu animato]:
> Brother! The inland mountain—Hath it not voice
>   and sound?
> Speaks not the dripping fountain
> as it bedews the ground?

Hers are the only songs I have learned to play by heart on the piano. I could never sing them for my children without getting a lump in my throat.

Nightly prayers were mandatory, with Mother presiding at the bedside. The litany was ecumenical and depended entirely on what she felt like singing at the moment. "Shema Yisroel" alternated with Gounod's "Ave María" and, my favorite, "Keep Me, O Keep Me, King of Kings, Beneath Thine Own Almighty Wings."

When Father accused her of religious inconsistency, she defended herself: "With prayers, there is no harm in being especially sure."

Oddly, the one part of Mother that did not change with the years was the purity of her singing voice. Even when she was in her eighties, once launched from her lips, the notes fluttered and flew about the room with the same old precision and delicacy. On one of our last visits together she said how glad she was that she had an untrained voice and that she had never learned to read music. This way she wasn't a slave to the rules. It was all done by ear and by instinct. If she heard a song once, it belonged to her ever afterward. Looking at a page of music, she could tell just how a measure ought to go, and she'd just "nail it up" with confidence. It is exactly, I told her, the way a writer, discovering the uniqueness of an object or an instant, "nails it" to the page with words. A tiny smile of fellowship was her reply, my reward.

Nobody knows how it happened, but Troy Music Hall had the most perfect acoustics in North America. It still does. A whispered aside from the back of the stage can be heard in the uppermost row of the balcony. It was no wonder that musicians and actors delighted to perform there. They could *hear* each other. In those days, small traveling companies of actors and singers passed through and were suitably awed. Only lacking was a curtain for the stage. For some reason, this was not considered necessary to achieve a "willing suspension of disbelief." A good part of the pleasure came from watching the scenery being changed between acts. Often this was done by the performers themselves. I recall that in a performance of *Rigoletto,* just prior to Act I, the Duke and Rigoletto, in full costume, carried a table to center stage, then proceeded to cover it with a gaily colored tablecloth. But the table was round, while the cloth was square and far too small. No matter how they turned it, the cloth would not fit. At last, the exasperated Duke balled up the cloth and tossed it offstage. What a shock of recognition when in Act III Rigoletto appeared carrying the dying Gilda in a sack identical to the misfitting tablecloth! Father hooted.

"Necessity," said Mother, "is the mother of invention."

It was at the music hall that I learned that some mysteries are meant to be deepened, not solved. The play was *Macbeth.* Between Acts I and II, Mother and I went backstage, and there, standing in her royal robes, was Lady Macbeth, eating a corned-beef sandwich! When she appeared later in the sleepwalking scene, scrubbing her hands and crying: "Out, damned spot, out!" I knew it was not blood she was trying to wipe away, but mustard. I have never seen *Macbeth* since without a touch of cynicism.

Once, when Billy and I were seated in the

balcony of the music hall and onstage in a large floppy hat Mother was in the throes of "What Are the Wild Waves Saying?" we heard two men whispering in the row behind us.

"Phew!" said one. "Too small the voice, too large the temperament." Followed by muffled laughter.

I could feel Billy growing murderous. Anything could happen. Turning, he leaned over and delivered it straight into the startled faces of the men: "You're pigs!" Then, to me: "Let's get the hell out of here." Once we were out on the street, my heart swelled with admiration.

"You should have died at that moment," I told Billy. "Never again will you be so ready to enter the Kingdom of Heaven."

"Will you shut your goddamn mouth?" he replied. It is no wonder that I followed him around like a dog. As for me, that was not to be the last time I would suffer at the hands of the unbeatifiable arbiters of taste.

On the stage of the Troy Music Hall Mother played the ingenue and was an utterly shameless scene stealer. Billy and I attended every performance. We wouldn't have missed it for the world. Family lore had it that, as a girl, Mother supplemented the household income by singing in the riverfront taverns of Montreal. What in the world could those illegal aliens from Poland and the Ukraine have made of the "Kashmiri Love Song"?

It was no secret that Mother did not share Father's love for Troy. Born and raised in Montreal, albeit in the ghetto of St. Urbain Street, she considered Troy a geographical come-down.

While I was content to let sleeping dogs lie, Billy never lost a chance to stir the pot of dissension.

"Why did we ever have to come live in Troy in the first place?"

"To start a new life," said Father. "It was the kindness of Fate that brought us here." Mother always took the bait.

"It was because that old Hudson automobile broke down halfway to New York City and there wasn't any money to have it repaired. We simply had to stay in this misbegotten town. As for the so-called kindness of Fate, I have already expressed myself."

"A thousand times," said Father wearily. Once in a while, a shadow would appear on his forehead, something that lay hidden until it was pressed to the surface. What could it be? A secret, I decided, threatening to come out in the open.

Politically, the town was overwhelmingly in the Democratic party. Our family was pro-Roosevelt, all except Mother who said her idea of a great leader was Arturo Toscanini. What sprouted and flourished during the Great Depression was bigotry. The most popular radio program was the weekly sermon delivered by the racist and fascist priest, Father Coughlin.

Mother was also the "doctor's wife," a position of no small importance in those days. People thought she knew more than she did. Not a day went by but she was stopped on the street and asked for medical advice, which she ladled out as if it were bounty. She didn't always get it right and a portion of Father's time had to be spent countermanding her suggestions.

"You cannot possibly be having nervous prostration," she reassured one woman. "That is a disorder of the male gland."

"No," said Father, setting about to instruct her in the difference between *prostrate* and *prostate*. "It is no easy thing to lie *prostate* upon the ground. Even for those of us who have one." So far as I know, such quibbling didn't cause her a moment's hesitation the next time she was asked for her opinion.

Aside from their sons, the two of them had no single interest or taste in common. The myth of the Selzer family was enacted in that house on Fifth Avenue in an atmosphere of affectionate exasperation and tolerant mendacity. Both of them kept secrets. As for the difference between Billy and me, let the twin beds in our room speak. In the morning mine bore scarcely more evidence of use than had it been occupied by a setting hen. Billy's presented a wild tangle of sheet and pillow as though he had battled the whole night long.

At the age of fifty, his wife having died, Grandpa Schneider retired from the sweatshops of Montreal and came to live with us. His baggage consisted only of the family samovar and the purple velvet bag stitched with gold Hebrew letters that held his phylacteries. I was three when he moved in, and I cannot remember living without the presence of that great potbellied silver appliance, which, by something like divine providence, had made it to the New World in the arms of the young immigrant. Enthroned on the buffet in the dining room, the samovar seemed always to be half alive, what with the bubbling noises and wisps of steam. Now and then, it expressed its disapproval by spitting on the rug. Again and again, drawn by the soft respiration of the samovar, I would gaze at my distorted reflection in its fat belly and enter a state of enchantment. It was like living with a benevolent wizard. Grandpa loved his samovar as he had never loved his wife, and spent a portion of each day cleaning and polishing and brewing. Every afternoon at precisely two o'clock, Grandpa would turn the spigot and pour himself the first of many glasses of tea, which, along with a weekly quart of rye whiskey, constituted his entire fluid intake. Then, inserting a lump of sugar between his gums, he sipped away the hours of contentment.

For the more than sixty years that he lived on the continent of North America, Grandpa remained blissfully stateless. The idea of citizenship never occurred to him, neither in Canada, which he had entered illegally, nor in the United States. Why would he need it? Like Louis XIV, he *was* the state. A tiny man with erect posture and a black Vandyke beard, he bore a striking resemblance to another king—George V of England. All but his nose, a large fleshy organ where resided most of his personality. Father never tired of referring to him as "His Majesty." Grandpa occupied a room on the first floor behind the office. Here the old king spent his days reading the Jewish newspaper through a large magnifying glass and wandering from his bed to his garden in the backyard. There he would sit for hours at a time in a straight-backed chair with a suit jacket over his shoulders like a military cape, one hand resting on his knee, the other stroking his beard as if pondering some grave affair of state.

Grandpa's English consisted of a literal phonetic spelling of the words on a page. Every name took on a Hebraic flavor. Billy and I tormented him with sticklers like James Buchanan, which became Zhamezz Boo-cha-nann. We found this hilarious.

"Never you mind those two," Mother consoled him. "You pronounced it perfectly. Besides, you are sweet. And they are not."

Royal though he appeared, he had the peasant's penchant for identifying people by their defects. Since it was often Grandpa who answered the doorbell after office hours, he would report to Father that Big Ears or Twisted Face was downstairs. An amputee was announced according to the part missing: The Leg or Fingers.

The population of Troy was predominantly Irish. Within a six-block radius of our house there were six saloons and six churches, each with its working belfry. On Sunday morning the windows had to be kept shut lest the quarreling of all those bells shatter sleep. They started ringing at 6 A.M. and didn't quit till late afternoon. Father said it was a holy war, what with the Catholics trying to drown out the Protestants and us poor atheists not being able to sleep.

Every house was equipped with an upright piano upon which someone was always practicing the scales. In warm weather one was transported from block to block "on wings of song." Mother used her own as an instrument of war, kneading the keys fiercely as if to make the music rise, all the while gazing up at the goblet of zinnias she had placed on top of the piano. When the notes did not require her full attention, she would sing snatches of song.

> The golden links of love are broken,
> Good-bye, you have back every token.

Rolling each *R* with relish and giving each vowel more weight than it deserved, she would deliver the pointed message to Father, who listened from behind his newspaper.

"That was lovely," he told her.

"I'm so glad you think so," came her sweet reply.

The house on Fifth Avenue was one in which an explorer might well make great discoveries. In addition to the Marquis de Sade hiding behind Gray's *Anatomy*, Billy and I had earlier found within an old wooden chest in the cellar a human skeleton that was or was not a patient that Father had murdered. And, on the topmost shelf at the very back of a closet in the attic, a shoe box that, when opened, gave off the faint smell of violets. What lay within, wrapped in tissue paper, was a fat coil of chestnut-colored hair more than three feet long. It was like coming upon a hibernating animal in its winter bed. Billy carried it downstairs and held it up so that Mother had to stop playing the piano and take notice.

"For Heaven's sake! Where have you boys been rummaging?"

"What is it?" We were dying to know.

"It's just my old hair. Here, let me see." She took it from Billy and held it up to the back of her neck. The end of the plait fell over one shoulder and onto her breast. It seemed to have a life of its own, the way it moved upon her body as though rejoicing to have returned at last to its native land.

"Whenever I took it all down and unwound it, I had a tent of fur. Nobody could see me. I might be sticking out my tongue at Aunt Sarah and she wouldn't know."

"But why did you cut it off?" It seemed worse, much worse, than an amputation. Mother shrugged airily.

"I did not want taking care of it to become my life's work."

"Why have you kept it all these years?"

"One day I'll sell it to the gypsies for making charms. Everyone knows that a virgin's hair can ward off evil spirits."

"I thought it was only a witch's hair. . . ."

"Put it back where you found it and stop that infernal rummaging."

A rope-driven dumbwaiter connected the examining room downstairs to our bedroom on the second floor. When there were no patients, Billy and I would send each other messages on it. Sometimes these were intercepted by Father who wrote his own reply. The shaft of the dumb- waiter was an ideal conduit for sound. Any words spoken above a whisper were gathered and transmitted undiluted from below upward. When it was discovered that Billy and I were eavesdropping during office hours, Father boarded up the dumbwaiter for all time.

The block of Fifth Avenue between Jacob and Federal Streets consisted of eleven houses variously made of wood, brick and brownstone. Not one of them but buckled and groaned in the several stages of skeletal degeneration. This was aggravated by the passage six times a day of the freight train that crossed the block near its southern end. Each time one came through, it was like living in Jericho with Joshua and all his trumpeters just outside the walls. It made Mother swear. She could always tell the Montrealer, she said. It whistled in the same key as "What Are the Wild Waves Saying?"

"Damn trains! A person cannot hear herself sing." As usual, Father turned it all to good purpose, claiming that the clicking of the wheels and the owlish sound of the whistle were sure cures for insomnia.

Each house was separated from its neighbor by a narrow gated alley that led to a backyard and each wore a balcony at the second story, giving the street the look of a colony of sluggish, one-eyed beasts. Next door to our house was an Episcopal church, which was attended on Sunday by a dozen or so elderly congregants but otherwise unused. Miss Olive Farnsworth was the organist, of whom Kinnicut, the punster who lived across the street, loved to remark that it was scandalous the way that old maid pumped out "hims" on the Sabbath. Kinnicut the Deplorable, Mother called him. Father said he couldn't help it: That was how his mind worked; it was a strain of madness peculiar to the Irish. Unconvinced, Mother would cross the street to avoid hearing that he never failed "to be dismayed on the first of June." Or that "with all due respect to Homer, it was the Trojan whores that *saved* the city of Troy."

"Vile man," muttered Mother, rolling up her eyes.

At the back of the house, there was a small flower garden with a bed of bearded white iris, another of lily-of-the-valley, two white peony bushes and a white lilac.

"White as death," said Mother, and planted half a dozen Oriental poppies. "Nothing like orange poppies to raise the temperature of a garden."

There were three trees on the block, two old maples, each of which bore large tumorous growths on the trunk, and a tall ailanthus—or stinkweed—whose crushed leaves gave off an unpleasant smell. At the northern end, the street widened into a cobbled "square" (trapezoid, really), in the center of which stood a circular stone horse trough. At any given time, this square was rich with manure and the resultant flourish of weeds.

Directly behind our house was an empty lot ideal for playing softball. During World War II the lot was divided into Victory gardens where all of the neighbors grew vegetables. In our plot Grandpa raised tomatoes for pickling. Five years later, before he died, Father and I helped gather the last of the crop.

"Leave the best one on the vines," said Father.

"Why?"

Whereupon he bowed deeply to the single beauty I had not picked. "It's an offering to Priapus, the god of gardens, so that next year he will bring about another goodly crop of tomatoes." It wasn't long before Billy found out that Priapus was also the god of erections.

"Between a tomato and a hard-on," he announced, "give me a boner every time."

Beyond the empty lot was the single block of King Street, lined with markets, a pool room, barbershop and the usual saloon. From there a crooked alley of cobblestones led toward the river. It was littered with garbage set out from the back doors of the markets on King Street—rotting oranges and cabbages, the bones of cattle and sheep, the excrement of cats, dogs and men. You had to keep your mouth closed against the flies, but then there was the smell. Here one-eyed cats and three-legged dogs scavenged; a hobo, not always the same one, would be lying asleep. Or was he. . . ? You had to step around him to pass.

Once I remember stepping right *over* him, fearing that he'd reach up and grab me, pull me down into his stink. Nearby, there was the remains of a fire. Once I saw the wind blow an ember toward the man's head, but he didn't stir, even when his cap began to smolder.

Holding up my fishing pole and can of worms, I would hurry past the condemned house all boarded up, from which came knocking sounds and moans.

In a tenement on the other side of the tracks lived Roger, a silent, smiling, thickset boy of about ten, a year older than I. He did not go to Public School No. 5 or to any other, as far as I knew. Word was that he was "simple," but I thought him mysterious and exotic. One day we came upon each other in the alley. We had never spoken before. After a moment's hesitation he took me by the hand to the outside rickety staircase that led three flights up to where he lived. No one was at home. I remember the meager kitchen with its old-fashioned stove and icebox, the plain wooden table and three chairs. Reaching into the icebox, Roger took something out, then turned and held it out to me. A single radish bloomed like a rosebud in the grime of his open hand.

"Eat," he said, smiling and nodding. It was my first radish. Crisp and bitter, it told the whole story of this boy's life. When, all at once, he put his arms around me, I broke away and bolted down the stairs. For days I kept the taste of that radish in my mouth. I have never liked them since.

All day long trucks and carts, some still horse-drawn, crawled up and down the streets, each laden with its product: watermelons, apples, milk, bread, fish, eggs. What with the ragman calling out "Raa-haags!" the cries of the knife sharpener, key maker, the iceman and the coal man, someone was always hollering for attention. Father made it a point to buy something from the vegetable truck whether we needed it or not. His mother had sold cucumbers from such a horse cart in the Ukraine just before he was born. He could almost remember the jouncing, he said. The pure liquid sound of hoofbeats on the cobblestones struck everything else dumb. Muffled were all the groans and coughs. I never tired of watching the sumptuous lashing of their tails, the gloss on their rumps, their womanly legs. How, without the horse breaking stride, its black anus would bulge open and deliver one, two, three tawny balls to make a golden loaf, then blink shut. Moments later, the daring sparrows were at their feast. One day the old breadwagon horse lay down in the middle of the square near the trough. No amount of slapping or cursing would coax him to rise. After an hour or so, he died. All afternoon we watched the struggle to hoist the corpse onto a dump truck.

"Pathetic," said Mother.

"Heroic," said Father.

Billy had the last word by reciting from Sir Walter Scott:

> For the good steed, his labors o'er
> Stretched his stiff limbs, to rise no more.

Years later, home from medical school, I saw that the trough had been removed and the site patched with blacktop. Shame on you, Troy! The replacement of the horse by the gasoline engine in no way justifies the dismantling of so wondrous a thing as a horse trough, whose reason for being was as much the delight of children as it was the slaking of equine thirst. Why not have let it stand so that small boats might still be set sail in its cistern? And a child, gone muzzy with dreaming, might lead his ghostly stallion to the bowl's lip and gaze enchanted as, with mane awash, the great beast pulled water into its massive throat?

Tuesday was wash day at our house. Back then laundry was still laundry. It was done in two great sinks in the basement by the McGucken sisters, whom Father had long ago rescued from the House of Good Shepherd, a home for "wayward girls." The linen from the office had to be boiled separately in a large pot, then fished out with a pole. Cheerful, raucous and hearty, Flo and Kate filled the basement with cigarette smoke and laughter, their voices calling out above the rhythmic rubbing of the washboards. What with the clouds of steam and the mingled smell of brown soap, starch and ammonia, it was a reenactment of Dante's *Inferno*. Best was watching them take down the sheets from the clotheslines, then send them through the mangle. The procedure seems to me now every bit as complex and dramatic as gallbladder surgery.

In the exaggerated stillness of summer evenings, the town clicked away. Insects clicked at the screens; there was the clicking of balls from the pool room on King Street, of Mother's ivory bracelets and of her fingernails on the piano keys, of the bead curtains between the parlor and the dining room, of Grandpa's dentures floating about in his mouth, of the wheels of the freight train crossing Fifth Avenue, of rosary beads when a pair of nuns walked by, of the reeds in the shallows at Watervliet, across the river from Troy, of a horse's hooves on the cobblestones when a wagon came down the street.

What with the river traffic, the railroad and our location midway between New York and Montreal, Troy was ideally suited for prostitution. Grumble and thunder as the clergy was wont to do every Sunday, whoring and its spin-offs were all that kept the town alive during the Depression. Every weekend men came from as far away as Plattsburgh and Poughkeepsie "to get their ashes hauled." It's a wonder the municipal plumbing stood it. In the pecking order of prostitution, the house whores were the elite. They were greatly outnumbered by the streetwalkers, who had seen better days and were now in thrall to their slitty-eyed pimps. A good many of the whores were local girls, who were generally mourned as dead by their parents.

The brothels were one block to the east of us on Sixth Avenue, and partly because of proximity, a good part of Father's practice was carried out among the prostitutes who worked there. At any given time one or more of them might be seen sitting in the waiting room on the first floor. Despite Father's repeated assurances that neither syphilis nor gonorrhea could be transmitted by sitting, Mother persisted in washing down the oak chairs with creosote every morning, all the while breathing deep sighs of damnation.

"Troy," Father told Mother, "is not Babylon. It is just a poor wretched town doing the only thing it knows how to do." To him it was vice devoid of viciousness. The worst that could be said of the prostitutes, he said, was that they were civilized women who, like a great many wives, demanded payment for their affections. To the annoyance of the Quebecois, he insisted on calling syphilis "the French disease." Father Quinn, on the other hand, revealed from his pulpit at St. Peter's that it was due to "demons begotten by fornication," which Father allowed was not a bad way to describe the spirochetes.

It was prostitution that caused me to be conceived in Havana, Cuba. Mother told me about it on my twenty-first birthday. One evening in October 1927 Father came upstairs from his darkened office and handed her two tickets for a cruise to Havana.

"And just where did you get those?" she asked suspiciously.

"Never you mind where I got them. Do you want to go or not? We'll leave Billy with the Kinnicuts."

"Which one of *them* was it?"

"Mame Fay."

"Mame! And where did Herself get them?"

"Well," he said, "they were a sort of payment for services rendered."

"Why doesn't she go to Havana, Cuba, herself?"

"Mame says she doesn't feel she can get away right now."

"Harlots cannot get away but doctors can? I cannot go to Havana, Cuba, on the ill-gotten gains of a courtesan." She never could bring herself to use the word *whore*. She felt it would only bring her down to *their* level. In the end they spent a week at the Hotel Nacional in Havana. Upon my graduation from medical school in Albany she showed *me* two airplane tickets to Havana, Cuba.

"Where did you get them?" I wanted to know.

"I've been saving up," she said unconvincingly.

"Are you quite sure they were not a sort of payment for services rendered?" That falling-water laugh. And so it happened that I was taken by her to the scene of my conception. When Billy heard about it, he said it was a wonder I turned out as well as I did.

While Nature in her wisdom causes most women to forget the pangs of childbirth, Mother held fast to each one of her ancient uterine contractions. All her life she was quite prepared to describe (to whomever—usually me) all the splendors of her agony in bringing me into the world. Needless to say, I found it embarrassing. Once I challenged her.

"Isn't it odd that while you can recall every kick and punch, I have no recollection of a single moment of my tenancy in your insides?"

"That's why the sweet little groove," she said, placing a finger from my nose to my mouth. "It is made by the shushing finger of the angel who cautions the new baby not to tell the secrets of life before birth." Not for her the great hallelujahs of childbirth.

"I had so wanted you to be a girl," she said. And blamed my regrettable passage into masculinity on Grandma Selzer, who had urged her during labor to struggle a little longer and bring forth a male child.

Sometimes she thought she owed it to motherhood in general to be unyielding.

"No you may not!"

"But why can't I?"

"*En français, s'il vous plaît.*"

"*Mais pourquoi pas?*"

"I have my reasons." And that would be

that. But not always. I remember that we were sitting on a great lawn that sloped down to a lake. I cannot remember where. Perhaps it took place in a dream?

"Tell me about Grandma Schneider?" I entreated her.

"Oh, she was one of those people who is forever holding out her hand to see if it is raining."

"Can I sit on your lap?"

"Certainly not! I am not the sort of woman who is always counting her children, now and then giving one of them a lick, another a cuff. Oh well then. Come on. But just for a few minutes."

Like many people devoted to their own opinions and prejudices, Mother was capable of high deeds, in the performance of which she was utterly selfless. To me, she seemed as valiant as Joan of Arc. Consider this:

It is ten o'clock of a summer night. The year is 1938. Father has taken Billy on house calls. Mother and I are standing in the bay window. Outside, the street is deserted. A woman, no longer young, rather matronly, turns the corner from Federal Street and walks down the block. She is dressed in a black suit and laced oxfords and wears a modest hat with a veil. A leather pocketbook is suspended from her wrist. Her stride is purposeful, as if toward some destination.

"*That* one," Mother says under her breath. A black Packard sedan approaches from Jacob Street. The woman slows her pace and comes to a halt within the spray of light cast by the street lamp directly in front of the house. In the light the skin of her face is paper white, pitted and bunched as from an ancient burnt-out acne. Slowly she opens her purse, removes a compact and begins to powder her face. To do so she must insert the powder puff beneath the little veil of her hat. The Packard slows down. Even before it has stopped, a man in an overcoat and fedora jumps out. The woman looks up coolly, ready to smile. In the next instant the dead white face is frozen in a mask of terror. She turns as if to flee. The man catches her by the arm.

"No!" she screams. "I didn't, Lucky. I tell you, it wasn't me!" But her voice is shot down by his fist like a bird in midflight. Now another man has joined them. They have left the motor of the car running, the doors open. Together the men punch and kick the staggering woman. Nine blows (I count them) until she falls. Two final kicks and they are once again in the car. Two doors slam shut and the car speeds down the block and disappears. From beginning to end, no more than half a minute.

"Come with me," says Mother. "You will have to help." I follow her down the stairs and out to the street. Between the two of us we gather up what they have left on the pavement and bring it moaning into the house. The woman's face is swollen, purple; her lip is split, her nose a shapeless knob. Even before Mother has finished wiping away the blood, the woman reaches up to feel her teeth, runs one finger over them, exploring.

"Don't worry, Goldie," says Mother. "They didn't knock them out." And to no one in particular: "They know how to do it without knocking out the teeth." Goldie! She knows her name! And that had been *her* name too, before she had exchanged it for Gertrude.

"Who are *they*?" I asked. "Why didn't they want to knock her teeth out?"

But Mother wouldn't say who or why. "Take a pail of water and a scrubbing brush. Go and clean that sidewalk. Do a good job." Outside, there is a silence as though the street had been cleared for the arrival of a hearse. I kneel and begin to scrub. Up and down the block, lights have gone on, curtains have parted. A man calls out. Someone coughs. A dog barks. I feel the eyes of the neighbors burning into the back of my head. My face is hot with shame, as though I had been caught in the act of public lewdness. Like the beaten woman, I want to cry out: I didn't do it! It wasn't me! When I have finished, I take the pail and brush and go to enter the house. My foot steps on something soft, like flesh. Oh God! Some part of her torn loose? But it is only the flesh-colored powder puff. I pick it up between thumb and forefinger. There is the faint, genteel odor of lily-of-the-valley.

The next morning the woman called Goldie is gone. I am in the kitchen moping over a bowl of lumpy oatmeal.

"I am never going to do that again," I say.

"Eat your oatmeal," she replies. "You'll be late for school." The severity leaves her voice. "Oh yes you will do it again," she says softly. "I am afraid you were made for it." And, as an afterthought: "If they ever decide to build an addition onto Hell, they can use this town as the model."

It was no longer a schoolboy who, an hour later, heard his name called and stood to translate from the Latin:

> The Gauls had tried every measure and as nothing had succeeded they resolved next day to escape from the town as Vercingetorix urged and ordered. They hoped that by attempting it in the middle of the night they would accomplish with no great loss of their men because the camp of Vercingetorix was not far from the town and the marsh must hinder the Romans in pursuit.

All at once, I hated that town full of whores and TB, its sooty air, the religious warfare of its bells, those ugly Latin sentences, those old-maid schoolteachers with their false teeth, the pimps with their killer eyes who knew how not to damage their merchandise. I would do as Vercingetorix had urged and ordered. I would get out of there the first chance I got, hop the night train to Montreal. And I would never come back.

In the fall of 1952, I was one of four second-year medical students who earned room and board by working nights at a hospital that bore the lugubrious name Memorial. It was a run-down place situated in the slums of lower Albany and its patients were drawn from among the slum dwellers. On hospital staff were four elderly, genteel Latvian-refugee doctors. They had exchanged the horrors of Stalin for the egotism and boorishness of the American doctors, who treated them as servants. Even though they had found themselves on the bottom rung of their profession without any hope of betterment, I never heard one of them complain or, as is the wont of so many exiles, mourn the passing of a better day. All four of them were unaccountably cheerful and sweet-tempered. With them, we four "externs" took our breakfast and dinner in the basement dining room, where the meals were cooked and served by a maniacal shrew given to bursts of rage in which she would fling the food about her and shout obscenities. During one of these outbursts, I commiserated with the Latvians, for whom this was a frequent experience.

"Never mind," said Dr. Pinkans, a woman. "It doesn't matter. Probably the poor woman has troubles of her own."

It was the duty of the externs to man the hospital at night. Mostly we assisted at emergency surgery, delivered babies, inserted needles and tubes and trembled. In the emergency room we hoped only not to kill anyone.

We were quartered on the top floor of a vast, unused warehouse at the rear of the hospital. From the tavern across the street throughout the night came a reedy tenor announcing the distant world of sexuality to which we aspired mightily but which remained forever around the next corner.

It was in the emergency room of that hospital where, summoned one night, I saw lying on a stretcher what had been a middle-aged woman, but now was unrecognizable as such because of the great deep laceration of her scalp and brow. One bloody eyeball protruded. She was breathing her last. Two policemen lounged at the nurses' station. Wiping the blood from her face, I asked them about her.

"She's from Troy," said one of the policemen. "An old hooker." O my Trojan women!
Andromache, Cassandra, Hecuba, Goldie. Moments later the woman was dead. Closing her
eyes with thumb and forefinger, I wondered
what she was doing way over here in Albany.
Mother was right. I *would* be doing it again.

Chapter 2

Every Sunday afternoon in July and August, we drove the twenty miles to Saratoga. There was abroad in the land the myth that its mineral springs did wonders to disimpact the bowels and otherwise bolster one's resistance. Grandpa swore by them. What with my car sickness and the further nauseating sight of Grandpa swallowing glass after glass of the turbid, malodorous bilge, each of these outings was a gastric martyrdom. Always on the scrawny side, I could turn alarmingly gaunt and drown in my hand-me-down clothes whenever I thought Mother's sympathies had wandered too far. But such a trick could not be used in the summer or, come Sunday, I would be forced to drink of the waters of Saratoga for my knavishness.

One Sunday we returned to Troy to find Second Street crowded with people and dense with smoke. The fire truck was standing in front

of our house, from the windows of which smoke
was billowing. There was the crackle of flames.
Even before the fire had been put out, Father
went inside to see. He emerged to tell us that the
house and almost everything in it had been either burnt black or ruined by water from the
hoses. Billy and I whimpered for our lost possessions.

"They were only things," Mother said airily.
"Things do not matter."

Father was disconsolate, for he had lost his
old black doctor's bag. Scuffed and with its handles drooping like the ears of an old hound, it
had accompanied him on his rounds for so long
that he had come to treat it as a pet, grooming
it with oil or black shoe polish, patching it with
adhesive tape or putting in a couple of stitches
to reinforce a seam that threatened to give way.
A few days after the fire, he came back from Albany with a shiny new black bag whose handles
stood straight up, alert and listening. It wasn't
the same.

"They were only things," Mother had said.
"Things don't matter." But I didn't believe her
then and I don't know. Things do matter. I
am not opposed to owning property. Property
is charming. A child clings to her doll or to
the frayed fragment of a blanket that has become dear to her by familiarity and association.
She has imbued it with comforting images and
sensations. She has every right to derive pleasure from it. In just that way do I cherish the
few possessions that have come down to me
from that house on Second Street, Grandpa's
eight-day German wall clock, for one. Some-

times now, about once a year, I give it a couple of turns of the key—about an hour's worth, and set the pendulum going. Then I listen once more to the loud ticking until the great bonging of the hour, which I can scarcely bear to hear even once. Each time, my hands fly up to cover my ears to block out the sound of my losses.

The greatest loss in the fire on Second Street was the samovar. The rubble having cooled, Father went inside the house to assess the damage. When he returned, he was holding the shapeless, melted-down lump that had been Grandpa's darling. He held it out to the old man, who cradled it in his arms as though it were the corpse of Cordelia while great tears ran down his cheeks. When Mother said for him not to grieve so, that she would get him another samovar, Grandpa turned on her with a look of fury and shouted, "No!" She knew never to bring up the subject again.

Of the four brothers and sisters with whom Mother grew up in the Montreal ghetto, the youngest, Herman, was the one she most dearly loved. She doted on him. As a young boy, Herman had been crippled by polio. One leg was markedly atrophic and shorter by four inches than the other. His spine, too, had been so affected that his body was bent to the right. With each step his head rocketed forward like a rooster's, then back. Slight, with dark sorrowful eyes and a rare smile of great beauty, he bore a resemblance to Kafka—the same triangular face. He and his older brother Frank had followed Mother to Troy, and together they ran a dry-cleaning shop on Hoosick Street. When, after a number of years, Frank married, Herman moved in with us. Within weeks he had become less an uncle than an older brother. Then came World War II and there were rumors that illegal aliens would be deported, or worse. It was decided that Herman should go back to Montreal until the danger had passed. Six weeks later, word arrived that he had died of pneumonia. His last words were from one of Mother's favorite songs: "Ah, sweet mystery of life, at last I've found you." He was thirty-one.

For days, the house was filled with Mother's grief. Like an animal that holds nothing back, she was beyond restraint or shame. There was no getting away from the sound of her wailing even with the pillow held over my ears. In the waiting room the patients listened and made the sign of the cross. In the street the people shook their heads and put out their cigarettes, the bread horse pricked up its ears. Day after day she lay upon the bed, her face blotted out, except for her open, twisted mouth, moaning. When the blankets on her bed recoiled, she neglected to cover herself. Father hung over her.

"Stop," he told her. "Try to stop. Make an effort. Look at your boys." But she could not stop, and refused the sedatives that again and again Father offered. On the fourth day, Grandpa, whose loss was as great as hers, laid a palm across her mouth.

"Sha! Shtill! Do you want to kill me?" he

asked. Whereupon she fell silent and rose from
the bed. It was over. She never sang that song
again. And I had learned the self-lacerating art
of concealing my grief, of drawing it down into
a tiny silver bead beneath the breastbone and
keeping it there out of sight.

Every October, Mother took the train to
Montreal to visit Uncle Herman's grave and to
walk on St. Urbain Street. A few days later, she
returned utterly refreshed. She was like that forest sprite who had been born in a well and every
so often dove into her birthplace to rejuvenate
herself.

Many times in the years to come, I would
stand in a hospital solarium where I had just given
out bad news to next of kin and listen to the hullabaloo of unabashed grief rising and falling about
me. Each time I would marvel at the honesty, the
utter shamelessness of such a spontaneous emotion. I have since had reason enough to fill my
own house with the sound of weeping but I could
not. From Mother's example it was to the decorum
of life that I was sentenced.

Behind the consultation room in the house
on Fifth Avenue was the laboratory, with its rich
pharmacy smell. Here, far into the night, Father
ground tablets with his gray marble mortar and
pestle, mixed, boiled, swirled, decanted and bot-
tled. Just beneath the doctor was an alchemist.
He loved concocting his own salves and syrups
on the copper sink top, where he kept a rack of
test tubes, a glass pipette and graduate, a funnel
and vials of many sizes. I came upon him once
adding a colorless fluid to a test tube that contained a white powder.

"What's that?" I wanted to know.

"That," he said importantly, "is the alexiphar-makon." I waited. "The antidote to all poisons," he explained. Then he dropped some crystals into the test tube, causing it to fume and over-flow. "There! Do you see?" And I did, until some years later, when I discovered that the ingredi-ents were sodium bicarbonate, potassium per-manganate and a chip of dry ice.

In addition to his practice, Father was the doctor at the Rensselaer County Jail. The jail-house was a yellow-brick building on the corner of Fifth Avenue and Congress Street. Inside, be-hind a receiving area, there were several long corridors lined on either side with cells. For years I died to be taken into that forbidden place with its hint of violence, the animal reek of confine-ment. It wasn't so much crime that filled the jail as public drunkenness. To Father, that was hardly a crime but the last resort of incompletely housebroken men in hard times.

"That is, if you don't count prayer," said Mother.

"Which I certainly do not," he replied. To-ward drunks, Father had something of the gen-erosity of the Japanese. Their presence made him lighthearted. He could not resist playing with them. To him they were holy fools.

"I don't nag them. It's a matter of tempera-ment, the booze, something passed on from fa-ther to son. Either you have it or you don't. If you do, it's in your tissues. Try to stay away from it and you can't."

There were always a few vagrant women at the jail, charged with "lascivious carriage." They weren't held overnight but were carted to the

House of Good Shepherd. Most of the time, I was tethered to the guard's desk outside the locked area. It was not until my twelfth birthday that Father invited me along. Once admitted by the latchkey, Father paused in the doorway for a few moments. One by one the prisoners became aware of his presence and stepped slowly to the bars of their cages like zoo animals coming forward to receive handouts from visitors. In addition to acute alcoholism, tuberculosis and the staggers of end-stage syphilis, the various degrees of delirium tremens, from the shakes to outright hallucinations, were what we saw there, along with the lacerations and contusions and broken bones that resulted from brawling, falling down or being hit by the enthusiastic billy clubs of the police. Feverish, filthy, trembling, the prisoners were docile and even good-natured. Had it not been for the bravado of whiskey, not one of them would have resisted arrest. Slowly Father worked his way down the aisle, entering each cell in turn, greeting the inmates with familiarity. With each, he enjoyed the same courteous little joke.

"A bit of a relapse, hey, Pat?" and "What! Dominic? You again?" It never failed to bring forth a shame-faced smile. Toward these men he was infinitely scrupulous, scrubbing his hands with soap and water between each examination, warming the cold metal disk of the stethoscope with his breath before applying it to a chest or belly, palming the disk so that his fingers and the heel of his thumb rested directly on the patient's skin.

"You want to touch them," he said. "Sometimes it's all you can do."

Those suspected of having tuberculosis were asked for a sample of sputum and sent under armed guard for a chest X ray. Once the diagnosis had been established, Father would try to coax the man into the Pawling Sanatorium in Albia, where bed rest, fresh air and milk were the only treatment. Streptomycin had not yet been discovered. For the refractory there would be pneumothorax, in which air was injected around a sick lung to collapse it and put it to rest. Or the even more terrible thoracoplasty, in which a number of ribs were removed to achieve the same purpose. It did not surprise Father whenever one of his "lungers" walked out of the sanatorium after a week or two.

"It is the *spiritual* calling," he said wearily.

What was it, I wonder from the distance of time, that turned all the strong young men of twenty to old rags of forty who played the numbers, abused their wives and lived on the dole? The more they drank, the less they ate, growing fleshless and bloated at the same time, with fluid collected in their lungs and ankles, bellies swollen with it, and some wearing the yellow livery of cirrhosis. It was the masochism of hopelessness, I think.

If Father valued any one character trait above all others, it was courtesy. He said it was the cornerstone of civilization. Punctuality, forgiveness, even world peace, were just offshoots of courtesy. In his more expansive moments, he would go so far as to attribute courtesy to other than human beings. The tree that tumbled during the hurricane and missed the house by inches was "the politest tree of my life." There was nothing more considerate than a squeaking door, he said. No matter what folly is being committed behind it, such a door gives misbehavior a moment or two to put on a face and straighten its clothing.

"You can't imagine," he said, "how many divorces a door has prevented by simply having the decency to squeak. Anyone who comes near the hinges with an oilcan better think twice." With such dogma ringing in our ears, it is no wonder that Billy and I developed a somewhat airy notion of sin. At the same time, we were exhorted not to become sneaks. Furtiveness is unattractive and anyway you always get found out. Better to wear your sins on the outside, where they can be seen, rather than inside, where they are far more likely to be rotting away.

Mother took a dim view of these sermons. "You're going to raise a couple of common fornicators," she scolded.

"Somebody has to do it," said Father. Years later, recalling all this, Billy said she was half right: He did raise a couple of fornicators. But nobody could say we are common.

If Troy was full of prostitutes, it was equally full of virgins, what with the large numbers of nuns and old maids. The only married teacher at Public School No. 5 was the man who taught shop. And he was a Protestant from Poughkeepsie. Supposedly out of earshot, Mother and Father debated the issue. She attributed it to an inbred brutishness among the male populace. They were unfit for commitment to home and family. And then along came the drink and it was too late. "And besides, there are the harlots."

But Father said that had nothing to do with it at all. It was the fault of a celibate clergy telling everyone else not to fornicate. The minute a man felt the least bit of desire, he had to give himself a slap in the brains or there'd be hell to pay. No wonder the population was going down every year, he lamented. The people had forgotten how to *do it*. When you didn't use a part of your body, it atrophied from disuse. That was nature's way.

It was less a connubial debate than an exercise in mendacity in which each played the role assigned. Whatever their true domestic drama, it was not naked but clothed in civility. Whatever their secret disappointments or resentments, each of their mouths was closed upon a pill of silence. In any case, Father needn't have worried about Billy and me letting things alone to atrophy.

Father hated ostentation. When the scion of the family that owned the detachable-collar factory parked his brand-new Packard in front of the house, Father was mortified lest anyone think it was his.

"They ought to bring back the sumptuary laws," he muttered. "Throw the fool in jail."

How to explain to the riverless child what a river is? Imagine green and silver in motion, you tell him. Now add a dog's tongue slowly lapping. But what is the real use of a river? he interrupts.

For those who live on its banks, a river is time itself, approaching, surging past, vanishing, never to be called back. You can tell your secrets to a river. It just carries them away. The elderly can sit by its water and weep for the passing of a better day. A river is for naked boys to dive into and revel in, to cast their sperm, then watch the fish rise to feed on the pearly flocculus. Then, too, there are the lisping of the reeds in the shallows off Green Island and, cocked on a lily pad, a frog on the *qui vive* for whatever might fly within tongue-shot. And swans, vain as surgeons, never out of sight of their reflections. Imagine the river at night, when strange creatures are summoned up from the bottom to float among the twisted vines of water, taking the moon on their cold scales.

What a dragon, that river! Every spring we had to feed it a youth or two just to keep it from going on a rampage. Once it was my playmate Leo LeBeau, who lived by the railroad tracks. At the funeral the priest spoke of drowning as the baptism after which there is no further sin.

"Stupidest thing I ever heard," said Father. But for once I could not be consoled by his pretense at cynicism. I had been reading the poems of John Keats and the epitaph he wrote for himself: "Here lies one whose name was writ in water." The next day I went down to the river, broke off a twig and wrote LEO LEBEAU in the stream, then watched the twig wobble out of sight. I felt better after that, as though Leo and I had shared yet another secret. A year into World War II, there weren't any youths left to offer, so the old dragon had to make due with wartime rations: a drunk who fell off a pier, the odd suicide leaping from the top of the Green Island Bridge.

By January the Hudson River hardened, its hibernant heartbeat no longer audible. Convinced of its solidity, we skated. But even then the pythoness would yawn in her sleep and a child fall among the hard bang of her teeth. Eddie O'Donnell was one of them. It was March when they found him, arms and yellow hair strewn, tumbling among the floes at Albany, the blades of his skates still flashing with the residue of exhilaration.

On the opposite bank of the Hudson (and reached by crossing the Green Island Bridge) stood the town of Watervliet, which, despite its proximity, was most emphatically not part of Troy. Aloof from the prostitution that sustained our economy during the dark years and gave to Troy the hectic glamour of Mahagonny, Watervliet was just another shame-faced gray village locked up in its own misery.

The river traffic was almost entirely commercial—tugboats, barges and small fishing vessels. Not yet polluted by the General Electric Company and others, but clean and pure, the Hudson, barely weaned from her Adirondack naiads, was teeming with edible fish—bass, perch, eels and even the rumor of sturgeon. While we saw plenty of eels wriggling on our fishing lines, only once did I see from the Green Island Bridge a huge dark shape moving along the bottom. Just the thought of those great slow sturgeon dining on dregs and laying caviar gave the river a kind of prehistoric opulence. Every few years, the spring rains and the melt from the Adirondacks were too much for the riverbed to hold, and the Hudson would lash its tail and come brawling through the lower streets, seeping into foyers, saturating carpets, dislodging benches and hat racks and purging the town like one of Mother's enemas, from which the devil himself deserved to rise purified. Each time it happened the children of Troy exulted. Who could resist the ruination, everything gone topsy-turvy?

"One year," said Father, "the water took the back door off its hinges. Next thing you know, a swan swam right into Grandpa's room, took a couple of turns around, hissed at him and departed. Isn't that right, Grandpa?"

"Judas Priest!" said Mother. "What next?"

When the flood came, no one thought of moving to higher ground. That was not our way. And so we stayed and watched the river licking bricks out of the walls, stones out of the street. For days on end the rain came down in sheets. From the kitchen window, the empty lot and King Street were a single lake. One time, through a scrim of rain I saw the figure of Christ walking on the water just as he had done at Galilee. I ran to get Billy.

"Look!" I cried, pointing to the apparition. "It's Jesus!"

Billy peered through the curtain of rain. "That," he announced in a voice dripping with disgust, "is no such thing. It's Old Man Sheridan standing on the roof of his Chevrolet."

"Don't tell anyone," I pleaded.

"I might and I might not," he offered, by which I guessed he would not.

Later I watched from the bay window as Father set out from the front porch to make a house call in a rowboat.

"Where are you going?" I shouted.

"Down to Washington Park," he called back.

"Can I come? Oh, please wait for me!" But, sitting in the boat, wearing his fedora and long overcoat and with a Lucky Strike clamped between his teeth, the bravest man in all Troy set out alone into the raging current that had been Fifth Avenue. Almost at once he seemed to be having trouble with the oars. At the corner of Fifth and Federal the two marauding streams turned incompatible and threw themselves into one another. With mounting horror I saw the little boat go tipsy and begin to circle in the maelstrom.

"I surely do hope it is not an emergency down there at Washington Park," said Mother. Then, as an afterthought, "He doesn't know how to swim."

Occupying the other seat in the rowboat was Father's black bag with its rows of pill bottles and jars of salve, each neatly labeled in his baroque handwriting: nitroglycerine; digitalis leaf; phenobarbital, half- and quarter-grain; tincture of opium; rhubarb and soda; glycerine and rosewater. As for the salves, there was Unguentine for burns, ammoniated mercury for impetigo and a black ointment called Ichthyol that brought boils to a head. And Father's own creation—Will's Foot Balm, named for my brother Billy. It was a specific for athlete's foot, the active ingredient being coal tar and a desquamating agent. It operated on the premise that since athlete's foot was a skin disease, you had to get rid of the skin. There was Beef, Iron and Wine for anemia. And a supply of mustard and turpentine for making plasters and stoups. Potassium permanganate for painting an ailing part purple. (I can think of no other reason.) Potassium chloride helped raise phlegm and, in a town full of tuberculosis, was in great demand. A compartment at the bottom of the bag held rolls of plaster of Paris, gauze and adhesive tape, a scalpel, scissors, forceps, metal probe, needle and thread, a rubber catheter, a few glass syringes, a test tube of boiled twine for tying off the umbilical cord and an alcohol lamp and a silver spoon for preparing injections of morphine. With such an armamentarium, what couldn't he cure? But mostly it was himself just stepping into a sickroom that effected the cure. He had that *je ne sais quoi* of all great shamans, an aura that informed his patients that their doctor was in touch with the secret powers of healing.

The people of Troy thought he could bring back the dead.

("Is it true?" I asked him once.

"Not yet," he said modestly. "I specialize in the half dead." And so he did, with injections of bee venom and jolts of electricity from his diathermy machine, a large black apparatus on wheels with wires, electrodes and a dashboard of many knobs.

"Someday he is going to electrocute someone with that thing," said Mother on more than one occasion.)

When, hours later, the little boat heaved

back into view, it contained, in addition to one exhausted general practitioner and his black bag, a blood-stained parcel in newspaper.

"Another damned chicken!" said Mother from the bay window. And so it was, freshly slaughtered: Father's fee for setting a broken wrist, applying the cast and suturing a laceration of the forehead. An old man, it seems, had fallen down a flight of stairs.

The day after the flood the sun came out. It was precisely then that Troy turned beautiful. Gone was all the sooty grayness; the peeling lack-luster buildings wore the rich patina of antiquity; the whole town and everything in it took on a kind of mineral splendor. It shimmered as though having risen from the pavement on a hot day. The men and women all wore halos. I mentioned it to Mother.

"Not only that," said Billy, "he saw Jesus on King Street."

"I thought so," said Mother. "We'll have your eyes tested." Two weeks later, with my new eyeglasses pinching the bridge of my nose, Troy was once again Troy and the dazzling uncertainty had vanished. It was the reverse of a glory. A happy conjunction of myopia and astigmatism had given the city that mirage-y look. O the cruelty of twenty-twenty vision that sees too much that exists on the surface and nothing of the *real* real that lies just beneath! As soon as I was out of the house, I took off the hated glasses and—presto! Troy was once again Ilium. Bare-eyed and squinting, I decided, was the only way to look at Troy.

Father's hero was Ambroise Paré, a six-

teenth-century barber-surgeon. Barber-surgeons
were distinguished from real doctors by "another stupidity of the church," the law that for-
bade physicians from shedding blood. After
three or four years spent dressing wounds at
a hospital in Paris, Paré spent the next thirty
years as a military surgeon attached to the armies of France. These armies were not
equipped with medical services. Each great noble was accompanied by his private physician.
The common soldiers doctored themselves or
used the barber-surgeons and quacks who followed the campaigns as adventurers. Like all
the surgeons who came after him, Paré learned
to treat wounds not from books but by trial
and error. Year in and year out, he fished for
bullets in the bodies of the wounded, amputated ruined arms and legs, splinted fractures
and dressed wounds, often under a hail of bullets on the field of battle. Nor did he refuse
the enemy his ministrations but treated them
with equal care. It must be so, said Father, for
a doctor's allegiance is to his Hippocratic oath
instead of to his king and fatherland.

Paré received no regular payment save what
the soldiers gave him: food, an article of clothing, wine, a horse and, once, a diamond straight
from the finger of a duchess for saving the life
of a nobleman.

"That's like you," I said to Father, "when the
patients give you a chicken or some fish or
apples."

"Yes," he said, immensely pleased, "like me."

Paré was a modest man. He refused to take
credit for his astonishing success at saving lives. "I

dressed him and God healed him," was his constant refrain. He was the most tender-hearted of doctors, again like Father, who told me of the time that the French army, after a long and bitter siege, entered a city, passing over the dead bodies and some not yet dead. Hearing them cry out under the horses' hooves made Paré's heart ache. After a while, he found a barn where he thought to stable his horse. Inside, he found four dead soldiers and three more still alive propped against the wall, their faces contorted with pain, their clothes still smoldering where the gunpowder had burned them. As Paré gazed at them with pity, an old soldier came up and asked whether there was any way to cure them. Paré shook his head sadly. Whereupon the old soldier went up to the wounded men and cut their throats "gently, efficiently and without ill will." Horrified at what he thought a great cruelty, Paré cried out to the executioner that he was a villain.

"No," said the man. "I pray God that if ever I come to be in that condition, someone will do the same for me."

"What else about Paré?" I wanted to know.

"Well," said Father. "Paré observed that because of their pain and terror and the noise of the battle, the wounded men could not sleep. So he induced sleep by making artificial rain. Everybody knows you can't stay awake with the sound of rain on the roof. He did it by causing water to be poured from a high place into a metal caldron so that the men might hear the sound of falling water and go to sleep."

"Like the freight trains?"

"Yes, like the freight trains."

Chapter 3

Except on Thanksgiving, when there was a roast turkey all garlanded with flowers like Ophelia's corpse, the culinary arts were given short shrift at our house. Everything was boiled to death and beyond—chicken, beef, potatoes, vegetables, fish, cabbage—all, all boiled. The sole genuflection to the palate was a gobbet of freshly grated horseradish that was applied to everything. If it can be said that one is what one eats, then I am a damp construction of boilage and horseradish. Somewhere about the age of ten, my appetite suffered a mortal wound and was borne away on its shield. It has never fully recovered, which accounts for my lifelong emaciation.

Mother was temperamentally unable to cook anything without lumps. Her oatmeal, applesauce and mashed potatoes were positively metastatic. To this day, I approach these dishes warily.

"Your mother is not one of those respectable women who likes to cook," she said. When speaking of cookery, Mother was given to referring to herself in the third person.

Every so often, Father contributed one of his own specialties of the house, such as his mashed potatoes. The potatoes were peeled, cut into quarters and boiled to perfection. In a large bowl, he hand-mashed them with a fork. From time to time, a dollop of clarified chicken fat was added. The product, he insisted, must be utterly smooth yet not runny. There was no danger of finding such a thing as a lump in Father's mashed potatoes; one spooned them down with confidence and trust.

His other specialty was "French" coffee. The grains were cast into a pan of boiling water and allowed to cook for ten minutes, after which the liquid was decanted into a second pan. An equal amount of milk was added, plus two tablespoons of sugar. This, too, was brought to a boil until a skin had formed to cover the surface.

In summertime the family diet was enlarged to include bowls of cold beef borscht into which scallions and cucumbers were sliced. At the last moment, a hot boiled potato was added, and, finally, a dollop of sour cream. It was, and has remained, my favorite dish.

Every few months relatives would arrive from Toronto, Montreal or New York City. Visitors rarely left before three months. Sometimes they stayed for a year. Grandma Selzer, for one. She was a tiny, neat woman whose gray hair was pulled cruelly back into a tight bun. She had the puckered drawstring mouth of the toothless, which could not completely stifle the suspicion that once she had been beautiful. Grandpa Schneider and Grandma Selzer never did take to one another and managed to keep a coolish distance. She sat all day long in the upstairs bay window; he kept to himself in the backyard. The one thing they did together was pray every morning. I loved watching him put on his phylacteries with an exactitude born of piety. Grandma would wait in silence until he was ready. Then, for half an hour the parlor was transformed into a synagogue with all those lovely antiphonies of reading and response, his deep moist singsong ornamented by the grace notes of her soft dry whispers.

To my knowledge, Grandma Selzer's entire diet consisted of grapefruit, farmer's cheese, rye bread and chicken soup. With grapefruit, she was thorough to a fault, scraping at the inside with her spoon until all that was left to throw away was a translucent paper-thin rind.

Considering the diet to which we were condemned the rest of the year, it was the equivalent of the Israelites' finding manna in the Sinai when Mother's older sister Sarah came from Toronto. "A green frog!" Aunt Sarah would exclaim each time she saw me after an interval of months. "Such a color!" And to Mother: "You give him nothing to eat, call yourself a mother." Aunt Sarah was an immortal cook. Cooking was her "heart," she said—although, since she was given to sprinkling her speech with illicit H's, I cannot be sure she didn't mean her "art." No matter, either one was correct. Ten years older than Mother, Aunt Sarah was short, fat and outwardly jolly but with an underskin of melancholy that caused her to sigh rather than just breathe. Mother said for us not to feel bad; Aunt Sarah was one of those women who cherished their sorrows.

Nectar and ambrosia could not have tasted better than her apple strudel, sour-cherry pie, honey cake and mandel bread, to say nothing of her stuffed cabbage, flonken and sweet-and-sour meatballs. From morning to night on baking day she would stand at the kitchen table kneading, her strong fingers pressing, punching, squeezing to test—was it too thin? too thick? too dry? Without looking up, she would sprinkle on a handful of flour or reach for the pitcher to add a little more water, then thrust her hands back into the wad of pliant dough. When it was just right, she would straighten up, wipe off the clots that webbed her fingers, mold the loaves and lay them out on a buttered tin tray, where they looked like unborn babies. Sometimes Mother would complain that Aunt Sarah was monopolizing her kitchen and they'd have a little tiff salted with sisterly insults. But then they'd sing together—"Rozhinkes mit Mandlen" or a number that translated roughly to "Sun, Thou Shinest on Everyone Else"—after which Billy and I were allowed one still-warm butterkuchen apiece.

My earliest memory of Father was of being carried in his arms, and the smell of him. Later in boyhood I would watch him pick up a sick infant with all the gentleness of a cat taking a kitten in its mouth, and think back with sensuous pleasure to a time when it was I whom he held.

Years afterward, when I mentioned this to

Mother, she said yes, he had that knack. "What a shame that human mothers cannot hold their young in their jaws. Surely it would make vacuuming a rug easier knowing one's child was in no danger of being sucked up." While Mother did no housework to speak of, she referred to it a great deal, a habit that gave her both the queenly and the common touch. Grandma Selzer found her approach to spring cleaning contemptible and never lost a chance to mutter about dirt and disarray, to which Mother retorted with a sniff, "I have better uses for the spring than cleaning house, thank you." And that was that.

It was a five-block walk south on Fifth Avenue to Public School No. 5. Every morning at precisely 8:15 I was picked up by the twins, Alice and Lucy, big chubby girls who lived around the corner on Jacob Street. "Dickeeee! Dickeeee!" they would bawl, filling the street with their brays and giggles until, mortified, I ran downstairs to shut them up. For some reason Mother found this daily summons exceedingly funny. At the first "Dickeeee!" she would cover her mouth and gasp. Had she known what we talked about on the way to school and what we might or might not have done in the backyard of their house, she would have been less amused. It was Alice who first suggested that we show each other what we had "down below," although, years later, she insisted it had been Lucy. Suffice it to say, there were any number of occasions in their backyard when I lowered my knickers and they their bloomers while we examined each other with immense clinical curiosity.

The children of Public School No. 5 were for the most part blond, blue-eyed and pale, which was impractical in a town enveloped in soot. Pale children show the dirt so. In the lower grades the first half hour of each day was spent taking attendance. Roll call was a feast of beautiful names: Fully half the girls' were tailed with an *een*. There was Maureen, Colleen, Mavoureen, Kathleen and Evaleen, along with a number of Bridies, Sybils and Bridgets. The boys were Liam, Conal, Conor and Patrick. And Patrick. And Patrick. And Patrick. Next to them, Richard sounded like the strewing of ashes on pavement. As each name was called, we were required to leap to our feet and recite a proverb.

"Kathleen McGuire!"

"A rolling stone gathers no moss."

"Patrick Logan!"

"Empty barrels make the most noise."

"Richard Selzer!"

"A stitch in time saves nine."

A mindless exercise in rote and obedience? Never mind—it was an incantatory ritual, nothing short of a system of belief by which we could live. In the sixth grade, a new girl appeared. She had the unfortunate name of Cleopatra Reilly. While the rest of us whose tissues were not "subtly spun" could hide our imperfections behind quite ordinary names, poor, pigeon-toed, frizzy Egypt stood naked in the gale and had to suffer daily the pain of odious comparison.

Public School No. 5 was a cheerless two-story gray-stone building with a concrete play yard in front. By some eccentricity in the pipes, the great corridor was frigid while the classrooms were stuffy and overheated. At the vicious bell whose clang marked the end of one period and the beginning of another, the children rose as one and filed into the corridor to stand in silence like the newly dead being shunted from one mansion to another until we should arrive at Heaven or Hell.

The classrooms smelled of chalk, ink and urine. The teachers were Irish spinsters who had obtained their certificates at Normal School, large bosomy women given to wearing flamboyant silk dresses with tiny lace handkerchiefs tucked into a sleeve. Given also to wearing toilet water. Each teacher wore the particular scent that was her trademark: lily-of-the-valley, gardenia, carnation. Ever since, I have agreed with Cicero that the woman smells good who smells of nothing. Miss Feerick was famous for her ability to look out the window while you were reciting, then say, "Thank you," in a way to let you know that you had performed abominably. Miss Vaughan, long after she had gone stone deaf, continued to call out "Silence!" from force of habit. Miss McTammany taught by the ruler and wore the perpetual glower of the archangel on the day of Expulsion. Mademoiselle Bouton, a Quebecois, taught anatomical French, acting out the phrases. *"Je m'hausse les épaules"* was followed by a shrugging of shoulders. *"Je me fronce les sourcils,"* and she wrinkled her forehead. Miss Foyle taught manners by requiring each boy to stand and bow to her, each girl to drop a curtsy while she sat at her desk as upon a throne accepting the obeisance of her subjects.

"No, no, Colleen. That was clumsy. And

don't twitch so." Then, rising from her chair, she would take a bit of her skirt in either hand, cross one fat ankle over the other, incline her head just so and, slowly, with infinite grace, sink precisely three inches. "There, now you must do it again."

Each desk had an inkwell at the upper right corner. It was considered honorific to be chosen to fill these inkwells from the large nozzled can labeled HIGGINS' ETERNAL INK. The pens were of tapered wood with detachable steel nibs. I never mastered the knack of controlling the flow of ink to the tip of the nib. The paper upon which I practiced the Palmer method of penmanship was always soiled with great blobs. It was an early lesson that ink has a mind of its own. It goeth where it listeth. So many years later, in the throes of writer's block or, like Flaubert, rolling on the floor in search of *le mot juste,* I long for an inkwell full of Higgins' Eternal in which to dip my pen and come up with just the right word. As for those recalcitrant pens, they put me in mind of Sir Walter Scott. How one day, while out hunting, he suddenly thought of the sentence he had been trying to write all morning. He quickly shot a crow, whittled a pen from one of its feathers and wrote it down in crow's blood. Once or twice I tried making my own ink from a formula in *The Old Farmer's Almanac* but it came out like weak tea and such was the prose it produced.

In those days the handicapped children were not isolated but kept together with the rest of us until the seventh grade, when the logistics of transporting them to and fro became too difficult. While this was occasionally disruptive—the unpredictability of their outbursts and all—it was never less than entertaining, and surely it promoted tolerance. It was expected that some people would "take fits" or be "deaf and dumb" or "feebleminded." For the most part, these afflicted children were models of patience, sitting quietly while the rest of us recited the particularities of the French and Indian War, rejoicing when we performed well, sharing our disgrace when we did not. I remember one Spanish girl who could neither hear nor speak, but whose gaze was more eloquent than any speech. All her ethnic ebullience shone forth from her dark eyes, which overflowed with the zest of expression. And I remember a boy with the vague helpless smile of someone who had misplaced himself.

As unrefined as were their pupils, just so exquisite were the teachers. They were, to a woman, hypersensitive to drafts, and only when the rancid odor of the unwashed reached the level of toxicity would the biggest boy in class be asked to lower one window an inch with a long hooked pole. It was another unsought privilege to be sent to the teacher's kitchen for her lunch tray while the rest of the class played in the schoolyard. More than once, for my sins, it was I who carried a tray of asparagus on toast or chicken croquettes and Jell-o with a nipple of whipped cream.

There was one black boy in the school. Clifford was handsome and had a beautiful baritone voice, with which he rendered "Old Man River" and Negro spirituals at assembly. He was also the victim of prejudice. Once, driven to wild rebellion, he dipped his pen and shook it at Miss Rogers. Higgins' Eternal Ink flew in gobs over her silks.

"You goddamned nigger!" she shrieked and slapped him back and forth, back and forth, across the face.

From time to time, the school was swept by impetigo, lice or pinkeye. Of the three, lice was the worst, for it involved mortification of both flesh and spirit, itching and shame in equal portion. No classroom but had its quantity of freshly shaved scalps, each with a bloody nick or two from the paternal straight razor. It was in the fifth grade that pediculosis struck home. O dire was the twang of Apollo's silver bow when he shot his crab-tipped arrows down upon my head! To have one's head shaved for lice was humiliating. One wished for death. When Father had finished, I looked in the mirror and was shocked to see how small my head really was, scarcely more than a doorknob. And cold! The sight reduced me to tears and King George V to a fit of cruel laughter.

"You look like a penis," said Billy in a burst of generosity. When, two days later, his own depilation took place, I had the ignoble pleasure of returning the compliment.

During the polio epidemic everyone wore a green cloth amulet called a scapular tucked inside shirt or blouse. These were rectangles of green felt bearing a white cross from the center of which blazed the sacred heart of Jesus. Unbeknownst to Father and Grandpa, Mother had gotten hold of two of these scapulars from the

McGucken sisters. When Father discovered them pinned to our undershirts, he gave her a look.

"It is just to please the McGuckens," she said. "And anyway it can't hurt."

Perhaps out of some notion that clothes make the artist-to-be, Mother dressed me in baggy knickers, thigh-length tan cotton stockings held up by garters, a beret and a loose black bow beneath my collar. Any departure from the uniform of poverty worn by the boys at Public School No. 5 was greeted with derision in the schoolyard, and mine would have drawn comment from the clowns at the circus. Even Billy joined in.

"You look like the sack of Troy," he said.

When I related the story of my martyrdom, Mother, herself given to wearing costumes—veils, sashes and feathers—was impervious. "I'm surprised at you," she said. "It is a mark of character to rise above the taunts of the rabble."

I took to feigning illness so as to be allowed to stay home. I had already mastered the knack of looking dangerously gaunt. Now I managed spells of labored breathing; I coughed hideously. Mother, fearing that I might be developing "a chest," began to knit furiously. I lay in my bed reading and listened to the clicking of her knitting needles.

"What are you making?" I asked.

"You'll see. It's a surprise." Two weeks later, she held up the surprise. It was a helmet made of heavy gray wool with holes for the eyes and mouth and a broad "skirt" that covered neck, shoulders and upper chest both front and back.

"What's that?" I demanded.

"It's a balaclava. They wear them in the Crimea."

"I won't."

"Yes you will. Not another word!" She pulled the thing over my head and twitched it into place.

"There. Now you can go back to school." The smell of the wool was suffocating and my head itched. Furthermore, it didn't fit; the eye-holes were not always over my eyes. In the mirror I looked like *The Man in the Iron Mask*. I hated it as I have hated nothing else since. The next morning Alice and Lucy took one look and screamed, first in terror, then in hysterical laughter. Dying of shame, I could not hold back the tears. The girls insisted on trying it on, each splitting her sides at the sight of the other. It is to the everlasting credit of those hefty, spirited girls that, in the ensuing weeks, no one dared poke fun at me in their presence. To show my gratitude, I taught them to say 555 in French.

"Cinq cent cinquant cinq," I repeated over and over.

"Sank sonk sank-on sank," they chanted in unison, and to that cadence we marched to school prepared to face the Cossacks.

It was Father who rescued me. One evening, I knocked on the door of his consultation room during office hours, an action forbidden under all but the most urgent circumstances. Once inside, I burst into tears and announced that I would rather die than wear that crown of thorns.

"It's just a kind of hat," said Father.

"This is not the Crimea," I sobbed.

There followed a long, pondering silence. All at once, he brightened. "It must be done delicately," he said in a conspiratorial tone. "Your mother has placed a good deal of faith in that hat. It has become her religion. We'll do it with her weapon—poetry." He then instructed me to learn by heart Tennyson's "Charge of the Light Brigade." Did I think I could learn it by tomorrow? Did I!

"Right after supper, I'll give you the signal. Put on the balaclava. For atmosphere," he added slyly. "You won't want to be crying either." I shrugged and raised my hands to show I couldn't help it. "Just you imagine you're right there galloping between the cannons to right and left. You might be scared but you won't cry."

By midafternoon of the next day, I had all six stanzas down pat. At the table, rigid with anxiety, I waited for the high sign from Father. It came. I rose to my feet, pulled the hated garment over my head and spurred my horse. I got as far as

> Boldly they rode and well,
> Into the jaws of Death
> Into the mouth of Hell . . .

when all at once she said: "Take that silly thing off and give it here." And that was that. I never saw the balaclava again, but months later there was a newly knitted afghan on the couch, some of whose colors made me think of the Crimea.

To this day I give thanks to Tennyson for the repetitious meter and the likely rhymes that made his poem easy to memorize.

In contrast to Billy, who made every room his own by merely setting foot inside it, I was shy and shrimpish. Upon entering a room, I would sidle for a corner rather than risk the exposure of the open middle. Part of this had to do with my wardrobe, whose wormy circumstances made me look like John the Baptist. It is to these years of unwelcome attention to my attire that I attribute my lifelong lack of interest in dressing up. No matter what I put on in the morning, by noon it has taken on the patina of burlap and begun to ravel. But the role of a surgeon in our society demands otherwise, and my desultory efforts to look presentable were a pitiful attempt to suggest decorum without ever living up to it. A long white doctor's coat covers a good many lapses of haberdashery. For this reason alone, I had chosen the right profession.

Both Mother and Father wished us to acquire knowledge and wished further that it be fun to do so. Grandpa excepted, we were a wordy lot, with every one of us wanting to have his say and saying it as elaborately as we could. From early on, we were encouraged to memorize poems. At age seven, I had in my repertory most of Robert Louis Stevenson's *A Child's Garden of Verses,* a haphazard of Longfellow and, of course, the lyrics to any number of Mother's English music-hall and French art songs.

"Stocking up for later," Father called it. "At seven, the brain is at its most retentive."

For once, they agreed. "Wax and marble," she said. "Wax to receive, marble to keep."

It was in the 1930s that the blood of Troy ran at its most epic tide—swift, full and wine-dark. Homer? We were besotted with it. The woman leaning from an upstairs window at sunset was Penelope scanning the horizon for a glimpse of Odysseus' purple sail. The policeman directing traffic near the schoolhouse was Achilles, his burnished shield in miniature. A line of barges on the river became the triremes of Agamemnon, pennants flying, the flash of gold from their oars. One year there was an eclipse of the sun. We all drove up to Prospect Park to observe it.

"Watch closely through the pinhole," said Father, "and you'll see Apollo draw his shield in front of him." His voice tightened with excitement. "Right this minute he's striding down Olympus. Can you hear it? The rattling of the arrows in his quiver?" Billy and I looked up to see the sun god, dark save for a rim of fire, coming down the mountain like the fall of night. Moments later, there was the dire twang of his silver bow. All the way home, the old Hudson automobile was full of holy dread.

"You'll want to learn Latin," said Father, "so you can write prescriptions. Physics and chemistry will keep you rooted in the real world."

Mother made no secret of her preference for the poems of Byron and Shelley. Each evening at the supper table Billy and I were invited to present a bit of information we had acquired that day or recite a few lines of poetry. These sessions turned into spirited contests in which Billy and I strove to outdo each other, contests that I invariably lost as he scavenged compulsively from the *Encyclopaedia Britannica*, while in my head there were not many mansions.

I was given to playing it straight: "*palfrey*—a small saddle horse ridden by ladies"; "*tumbril*—a cart with two wheels that is tilted for dumping." That sort of thing.

But Billy had no shame. "*Cameo*," he instructed us. "The word comes from the Arabic. It was what you called out when your camel ran away."

"Really? How very interesting," said Mother.

"Rats!" said Father.

One night Billy revealed to us that Bulgaria was a country famous for the ugliness of its women. When angrily challenged by Mother, he leaped to the shelf, pulled down Volume B of the eleventh edition of the encyclopedia and showed her chapter and verse.

"That must have been written by an Englishman," said Mother.

Once in a while she joined in. "*Taffeta*," she told us, "from the Persian. It is not a kind of cloth, as you might think. It is a soft noise." We never checked the dictionary to see if she was right. It would have been "rude" to do so. Besides, if she wasn't right about *taffeta*, she ought to have been. In addition to the encyclopedia, there was in our bedroom a nine-volume set called the *Book of Knowledge*. Once it had been ten volumes, but "Oman–Prentice" had long since vanished. Night after night Billy sat up in his bed reading aloud as from the Book of Ecclesiastes, one verse at a time, all the while delivering editorial commentary, until my exhausted brain collapsed into sleep. His favorite of the set was "Jay–Mortmain." It is the one volume I still possess: By some miracle it has defied destruction. Letting it fall open at random is a visit with Billy.

"'In Locri Epizephryii, there is a temple of Proserpine. In the battle at the River Sagras, ten thousand Locrians defeated one hundred thirty thousand Crotonians with great carnage.'

"'Samuel Marsh, a missionary who spent many years in New Zealand and wrote a book about his intercourse among the Maori.'" (Billy: "Oho! Marsh! So that's your game, is it, Marsh? Do as I say, not as I do.")

"'Marmaros, a desert country where beautiful Arab girls in gauze pantaloons were open to blandishment.'" (Billy: "What needst thou the black tents of thy people, when thou hast the red pavilion of my heart?")

"'Kingfish—see Opah.'" Alas, I never did see Opah. It was in the missing "Oman–Prentice."

Far into the night, Billy and I lay awake in our beds trading words the way other boys traded marbles.

"Colorado."

"Alabaster."

"Spikenard."

"Spikenard? What's that?"

"A sweet-smelling oil. Some woman named Mary, not the Virgin, poured a jug of it on Jesus' feet and wiped them clean with her long hair."

Much to Father's amusement and in deference to Grandpa, part of each Saturday was to be spent reading the Old Testament. Personally, I have always preferred the Apocrypha to the Pentateuch, whose cast of characters—David, Saul, Abraham, Isaac, Jacob and the rest—seemed an unprincipled lot. I have never recognized myself or any of my friends in the pages of that book. In addition to Abraham, who sent poor Hagar and her little Ishmael out into the desert without food or water, there was David, who lusted after Bathsheba and plotted to have her husband slain in battle. And Jacob, who cheated Esau out of his birthright. And so on. To say nothing of the testy deity by whom they were all ensorcelled, and whose thunderbolts were designed to teach a terrified mankind not to trifle with intellectual curiosity. Only Isaiah, who complained that his "bowels vibrated like a harp," and who likened his cramps to those of a woman in labor, approached anything near to human vulnerability. One couldn't help but have some affection for a prophet with spastic colitis.

At home we studied Hebrew and what Father called vocabulary. In high school we learned Latin, French, Greek, English romantic poetry—Keats, Shelley and Byron—and American history, with special emphasis on the French and Indian War, for some reason. And Greek mythology. Later there were physics, chemistry, biology and algebra. Of these, only physics was beyond my ken. Mother said she wasn't surprised; I had the wrong-shaped head for it. To this day, the one bit of physics that I vaguely comprehend, I learned not in school, but in the bathroom of the house on Second Street. At age six, told to take a bath, I filled the tub to the rim absolute, stripped and jumped in.

"It is Archimedes' principle! Eureka!" cried Father. And he proceeded to explain that the volume of water sloshed out of the bathtub onto the floor was equal to that of my body.

"If you get it, cry Eureka!"

"Eureka," I said, but without the exclamation point, as I was not then nor am I now entirely sure about this principle!

It was in the third year of high school that I met the teacher of my heart. Miss Buckley was a tiny, passionate woman with hair already white at thirty-five and with a face like hand-painted china. She it was who led us through the Sinai of syntax to the Promised Land of epic poetry. I was head over heels in love with her and spent the entire year trying to attract her attention. Although never once did she acknowledge my passion, I have reason now to believe that she was not blind to the shameless tap dancing and cart-wheeling with which I carried out her assignments.

"Write a synopsis of the *Iliad*," she commanded the class, "in fifteen hundred words." For a week, I revised and polished what I was certain she would translate as a declaration of love. A week later the papers were returned to us. At the bottom of mine were three exclamation marks in red ink and a note requesting that I see her after school that day. At last! I had won her heart. All day I wandered from classroom to classroom like one besotted. Would four o'clock never come? At her desk, Miss Buckley was waiting for me. Be still, my heart, I thought.

"What a clever boy you are," she said. "I'm sure you will turn many a teacher's head before you're through. But not mine. Now hear this. You have twenty-four hours to do the assignment, which, unless the gift of memory has deserted me, was to write a synopsis of the story of the *Iliad*. Airy persiflage is not what I asked for."

Years later, I received word that she had died. Then, mailed to me by her next of kin, the very composition for which she had chastised me and which she had saved all that time. Reading it now, I cringe to think of all the airy persiflage I have committed to paper since. But that she had saved it!

Within the demanded twenty-four hours, I carried out the assignment she had given. Now, forty-five years later, I offer it to whatever of Miss Buckley is still reachable:

> Lately, I have been mulling over the Trojan War. My sympathies have always been with the Trojans. Leaving aside that I am one of that tribe, those ancient Greeks have always seemed to me an army of brats—a vain, sulky, sly lot. Take Ajax, for instance. When they wouldn't give him Achilles' armor after that one had gotten himself killed, he threw a tantrum and ran around slaughtering all the sheep he met up with under the delusion that they were so many Greeks. Then there was Agamemnon, who did not shrink to sacrifice his young daughter Iphigenia to the gods in order to secure calm seas for his fleet. Admittedly, fatherhood, unlike motherhood,

is an acquired taste, but still . . . At the last moment the goddess Diana substituted a hind and stole Iphigenia away to Taulis to be a priestess in her temple, which may or may not have been a worse fate. No credit either to that schemer Odysseus, who did everything on the sly. Consider only that he declared himself insane in order to get out of military service (it didn't work), cheated on his faithful wife, Penelope, every chance he got and brought about the fall of Troy by building a big wooden horse, filling it with men, then parking it outside the gates of the city. We Trojans, being as curious as raccoons, dragged the contraption inside the town to see. Whereupon the damned Greeks jumped out and set fire to Troy. And the rest, as they say, is history. The only decent one of the lot was Patroclus, who was Achilles' best friend. (Some say more.) After both Achilles and Patroclus had been slain, their bodies were cremated and the ashes mingled in the same urn, which I find rather sweet.

I much prefer the Trojans: Hector, Cassandra and the pious Aeneas, who survived the sack of the city and carried his old Daddy, Anchises, on his back to safety. Of all the Trojans, Cassandra is my favorite. She was so beautiful that Apollo himself fell in love with her. Although it must be said that he fell in love with a different mortal woman every Monday, Wednesday and Friday. (Of such tinder was his heart.) In return for what we used to call "her favors," Apollo granted her the gift of prophecy. But when, at the last minute, Cassandra said on second thought she preferred not to, the enraged god added on to his "gift" that, yes, she could still foretell the future but that nobody would believe her.

As for the Trojan War itself, the whole thing was engineered by a rotten little goddess named Discord to whom peace and quiet were bad news. She wasn't happy unless she was stirring a pot. A regular cooking-spoon of a goddess, Discord arranged a contest to determine which was the most beautiful: Venus, Juno or Athena. She threw amongst them a golden apple inscribed: *To the fairest*. Well you can imagine the ruckus up on Olympus—feathers and ichor all over the place. At last, a young Trojan shepherd named Paris was chosen to be the judge. Naturally, bribery ensued; shepherds, like politicians, are famous for being susceptible to it. Venus won hands down since she promised Paris the most beautiful woman in the world for his own, while Juno and Athena dangled only such abstractions as art, science and grandeur. In order to fulfill her part of the bargain, Venus sent Paris off to Greece, where the beauteous Helen, the wife of Menelaus, fell in love with him. Paris, it must be said, behaved badly as a guest at Menelaus' palace. Like many of us Trojans, he was incompletely housebroken and ought not to have been invited anywhere there are good carpets on the floors. The first chance he got, he kidnapped Helen off to Troy. (It was not exactly against her wishes.) Menelaus was irked. And that's how the whole silly business got going.

So thorough were the Greeks who sacked Troy that for thousands of years no one knew where it had stood. Until along about the middle of the nineteenth century, a German archaeologist named Schliemann announced that he had found the site, and he employed an army of Turks to dig the city out of the ground. Don't you believe it. I have no idea what it was that Schliemann unearthed, but it wasn't Troy. The real story has to do with Apollo, who, bored to death with his immortality and incapable of keeping his hands off mortal affairs, caused (who knows why?) the city to be rebuilt two hundred years ago on the banks of the Hudson River midway between New York and Montreal, where it stands to this day. That business about the Dutch having founded it is a snare and a delusion. It turns out that Cassandra was right after all.

"Wheel round your horses, Greeks," she exclaimed. "Your conquest is ill-favored. Troy will live again."

While I recall none of the events of the French and Indian War, I do remember the poems of Poe, Kipling and Longfellow, whose rhymes and effects, like those of Tennyson, were so predictable as to be easily committed to memory. I was intoxicated by them. Certain lines, read aloud, made me dizzy. This, from Poe's *The Raven:*

> The silken, sad uncertain rustling of each
> purple curtain.

And from Byron:

> The Assyrian came down like the wolf on the fold,
> And his cohorts were gleaming in purple and gold.

I was partial to poems with a distinctive martial ring, poems of feud and fight such as the one about Lochinvar, who kidnapped the bride of Netherby just before she was to be married to someone else.

So daring in love, and so dauntless in war,
Have ye e'er heard of gallant like young Lochinvar?

Who wouldn't die to be just like him? And in me, Sir Walter Scott found his ideal reader.

The stag at eve had drunk his fill,
Where danced the moon on Monan's rill.

I had only to look off into the distance to see the great beast lift his rack of antlers, muzzle dripping with water from the mountain stream whose tumbling surface reflected a *dancing* moon. And, of course, from the *Iliad,* Apollo's deadly arrows:

O dire was the twang of his silver bow.

For all of this, I thank the gallant women who spooned these poems into me, where I was to keep them next to my heart forever.

Chapter 4

From early on, I loved going with Father to St. Mary's Hospital. Actually that was its nickname, short for St. Mary, Consoler of the Afflicted. Or as Father liked to say, and made me say it too, Maria Consolatrix Afflictorum; he was of the conservative branch of atheism and insisted on the Latin. The hospital was a three-story red-brick building built in 1914, a long rectangle with two pavilions, or wings, extending from either side. Since it was operated and staffed by the Sisters of Charity, the building was winged in more ways than one. St. Mary's was situated halfway up the slope of a steep hill, from which you could look down over the town. Ever since, I have always thought that halfway up a hillside is just where a hospital belongs, midway between a cathedral on the top and a jailhouse at the foot, in touch with both the sacred and the profane. Whether it was prophetic or simply a matter of logistics, the cemetery was right up the street. From the hospital's solarium on the second floor you could watch the smoke from the crematorium chimney rise and diffuse over the city as the dead insisted upon mixing with the living. In summer, with the windows open, you could even catch a whiff of it, a compelling early lesson in death, resurrection and ecology. I can still close my eyes and smell that blend of starch, candle wax, ashes and roses that permeated St. Mary's Hospital. It is an odor that I have not smelled since in any of a lifetime of hospitals; it is the odor of sanctity, I think.

The nuns ran the place as though it were the flagship of a fleet on the eve of a naval battle. Here, if nowhere else, cleanliness *was* next to godliness. The polished floors wore a perpetual fanatic gleam, dirt was rooted out as though it were sin. It would take more than mere senility to make me forget Sister Michael's evening inspection of the long marble corridor. Behind her limped a wretched porter, who had spent the entire day washing and waxing the floor. I remember the stiff white wings of her cornet slicing the gloom, the crusader's curve of her nostrils, her eyes that reconnoitered every corner, then turned upon the miscreant with the glare of black olives as she pointed to a bit of smudge that was invisible to me. I remember how the Nun of Wrath aimed one bony finger at the spot for the poor devil to see, how he stood there with the good-for-nothing look of a dog that has just made a mess on the carpet. With the student nurses, she was equally exacting. Like that precise princess in the fairy tale, the one who was put out of sorts by a rose leaf out of place in the garden, just so did Sister Michael appear in the doorway of a ward, sniff once or twice and go directly to the very bed where one corner of a sheet had not been tucked to ferocity.

The habit of the Sisters of Charity was black, full and fell to within an inch and a half of the floor. From a cord about the waist, a black rosary hung. The wimple was topped by a starched white cornet with a broad lateral flap on either side of the head. One alone was a sailboat, two side by side a regatta, three a whole armada. These sisters did not walk; they skimmed, they hovered. Free of the drag of gravity by which the rest of us are rooted to the earth, they floated quickly and noiselessly, save for the soft click of wooden beads tossing among the folds of their habits. With each step, the black nose of a shoe would peek from beneath the hem then dart back inside the flaring recesses as though each of them were sheltering a family of mice.

More than once in the springtime I sat in the many-windowed solarium that was filled with vases of lilac and peony and gazed down the long hall in full expectation that the very next thing I would see coming toward me would be Maria Consolatrix Afflictorum Herself, to whom I would, oh yes I would, hold out my wounded heart. One evening Father came to collect me there.

"What were you doing?" I asked him.

"I was bringing a baby boy into the world," he replied. That's the way they used to talk in those days.

"Where did you bring it from?"

"A sealed garden."

"How did you get in if it was sealed?"

"The gate was opened just long enough for me to reach in and take him out. *Next subject*."

I opened a new line of questioning. "What is the Holy Trinity?"

"It's just an expression."

"No, what is it really?"

"It means the three who are one."

"I don't get it," I told him.

Father thought for a long moment. "Well, look," he said. "Here we are walking this corridor. Do you see those three wall lamps along the way? Let the first one be the Father, the next one the Son and the third the Holy Ghost. Each lamp gives out its own light but as we walk down the hall passing from one light to the next we still get some of the light from each one no matter where we are standing. Now do you get it?"

"You made that up."

"Then shut up," he explained. It is fifty years later, and as for the Holy Trinity, I still don't quite get it, but of all the explanations I have been given over the years, Father's makes the most sense.

At St. Mary's, the beds were lined up along the walls of large ward rooms. In time of need, a movable curtain screen could be placed so as to conceal the newly dead or to afford, if not privacy, at least the implication of it. To this day I am of the opinion that private rooms are a wrongheaded idea. Once encaged in a private room, the patient is out of sight as well as alone. This cannot be as safe or as functional as a great ward with fifteen beds lined up on either side, over which one sharp-eyed nurse can keep constant surveillance. To say nothing of the lovely commiseration that prevails in a ward and the hustle-bustle that is the antidote to the boredom of the bedridden. What architects and doctors have lost sight of is the pleasure the sick take in just plain gossiping. It is on a ward, not in a private room, where the craving for gossip is more likely to be satisfied. Besides, unless the gift of prophecy has deserted *me*, a ward is not one inch farther away from Heaven than a private room. When the time comes for me to be put to bed in a hospital, let it be in a ward, where my sighs and groans can mingle with the sighs and groans of my fellow human beings in the consolation of fraternity, and where it might be given to each of us in turn to utter the most beautiful sentence in the English language: There but for the grace of God go I.

As severe as Sister Michael was with the porter and the students, just so kindly did she move among the sick. Mercy, just before leaving the world of medicine forever, lingered awhile among those nuns. How different those sisters were from the doctors, who stepped importantly among the puddles of patients, especially the surgeons, each of whom was quite convinced that once he had left the ward his disembodied radiance lingered on. Father was the sisters' favorite. Their affection was based on his good-humored teasing, to which they responded with a commotion of cornets and a rolling up of the eyes. With what wit and gallantry he returned to those laborious virgins a glimmer of their long-forsworn sexuality. Temperamentally unable to surrender to faith myself, I have remained in a condition of awe at the faith of others. It is what constitutes for me a belief in God, only once removed, like a cousin. When I was twelve Father lay dying in St. Mary's Hospital. Long before my eyes had had their fill of him. I remember the vigilant nuns grouped like lamps in the darkened room, his face graying away, theirs glowing with an imperturbable golden light.

Years later, during summer vacations from college, I worked as a night orderly at St. Mary's. It was on my first night of duty that I was told to wheel a stretcher from the emergency room to the operating room and to go as quickly as I could, for the cargo in my charge was a young woman who, I was told, was hemorrhaging briskly. With one hand holding aloft a bottle of saline solution and the other pushing, I set off at a speed just short of reckless endangerment, only to find that the single working elevator was in use. When minutes went by, or hours (what does it matter how long?), and still the elevator didn't come, I began to despair for the life of my patient. From the head of the stretcher rose moan after moan to break the heart of Caligula. Was the red stain on the sheet spreading? A sister arrived also to wait for the elevator. At last, from the upper regions of the shaft, I heard the door slide shut, the gears engage and the car set in motion. Like a sentry on the alert, I prepared to storm and capture that elevator and rescue my first patient from certain death—only to watch as the empty car passed sluggishly by without stop-

ping. Its slow disappearance from view remains
one of the most sickening events of my life.
Again and again I kicked the door and pounded
it with my fist and I cursed it much as Jesus
cursed the fig tree that bore no fruit. Goddamn
elevator! I cried aloud. May your cables rust,
your gears be stripped, your door go unhinged
so that never again shall you know the bliss of
ascension or descent. To all of which the sister
responded with one of those sad little smiles
those people keep in their repertoire. Then she
reached for her beads and began to *offer it up.*
That nun hadn't got past bead one when the elevator appeared out of nowhere, and we all rose
to a happy ending. That was the trouble with
working at St. Mary's. You were always at risk of
having Her called in on consultation, which kept
a permanent sheepish expression on the faces of
the heathen.

From St. Mary's on, like the gaucho who
spends half his life on horseback, I have spent
half of mine inside a hospital. That is bound to
affect the way one perceives such a place. Lacking the least knowledge of architecture and unable to read blueprints, I have now and then
built a hospital in my mind.

I have a son, Jon, who makes metal sculp-
tures in the garage. What with his worktable,
tanks of acetylene gas, the hoses from which
spurt jets of bluish flame, and the piles of dere-
lict iron, steel, copper and brass, I have to leave
my car out on the street. Believe me, I am glad
to do that. For no mere automobile, were it a
Rolls-Royce done in gold leaf or my Chevrolet

at the height of its decrepitude, can match the
solidified dreams that issue from Vulcan's cave:
little dancing frogs made from coat hangers, a
giant bumblebee from a bag of tenpenny nails
and even a red-tailed hawk out of what, in a former life, had been horseshoes. Just so does a garage become a temple of reincarnation. Again
and again, the tongs and metal are thrust into
the flame, then hammered or bent to suit. From
time to time, a shower of sparks flies up in cele-
bration. Only last spring, he made a set of wind
chimes out of some old copper pipe and plaques
of tin weighted with lead. If my years be Methu-
selan, I shall never forget how, goggled and
aproned, he emerged from his forge holding
aloft those wind chimes. When, at precisely that
moment, a breeze took the chimes and I heard
for the first time that sweet confusion of notes,
it was as though a lamp had been turned on
somewhere deep inside my ear.

Surely, there is no more beautiful object
made by man than wind chimes, a thing born of
metal, of fire, ravishing equally to the eye and
ear, whose spatial configuration is no mere geometry, but geometry that at any moment may
be galvanized into life. Unlike the ticking of a
clock, the voice of wind chimes is not Swiss, that
is to say, automatic and regulated, but pagan, in
that it is dependent upon the surprise of streams
and currents of air. The soft concussion of its
parts cools the heated mind, inviting it to reverie.
Ever since Jon made them, the wind chimes hang
outside the back porch, near the kitchen, animating the paralytic old house, offering it the dream
of movement; at any moment, the house with all

of us in it might rise into the air as though it had been painted by Chagall. Thus has space been mastered and inertia overcome by the artist using nothing but fire, wind and earth. At night, lying in my bed, I wait to hear its soft palaver like a blind man who cocks his ear to hear the stars come out. There! It begins! And I am filled with a sense of harmony with the natural world. I am once again a pagan, for whom every tree, waterfall, rock and cliff is inhabited by spirits.

Just as I would never again live in a house without wind chimes, I would not call a building *hospital* that did not have a fountain on the premises. Were I to design a hospital, I would cause it to be built around a large reflecting pool, from the center of which would rise a fountain. Let it be a tall fountain with a powerful upward thrust and, at descending intervals, lateral leaves or petals to catch the fall, breaking it into a thousand secondary and tertiary *cascatelli*. There can be nothing so consolatory to the sick as a fountain. To such a waterfall, the sufferer will attribute all the antidotes to his symptoms. The mere contemplation of such a sympathetic element—water—leads naturally toward the ideal of recovery. Each night, with the fountain stilled, the sick and those who tend them might watch from their windows as Cassiopeia and Orion are enticed into the pool, glittering evidence of the celestial connection with earth. For those who cannot get well, a fall of water, by offering its destiny in full view, teaches the incurable how to die. Falling water knows how to comply with death by surrendering its voice, place, shape and identity to peaceful horizontality. It is the same complicity that wood has with the flames that devour it.

My hospital would face west. Before drawing the first line of my blueprint, I would imagine the building at sunset, those few minutes when it shows its true color—red, as though the building itself were hemorrhaging. Moments later, with every window ablaze, it becomes a crucible in which a core of radium is glowing. Hemorrhage, irradiation—these are events not unheard of within the precincts of a hospital. At noon, the building would resemble a great supine human body, its corridors a labyrinth of arteries circulating corpuscles of light to every corner. At such times—sunset, noon—a hospital is transformed and exalted by the elements. And so water and sunlight must not be underestimated any more than the architect would ignore the lessons of brick, wood or glass. What is brick, after all, but the earth taken up, molded and burnt in the fire? Each brick is a fragment of the planet, wrested free, purified, then placed in precise juxtaposition to its fellows. What is wood but a creature that was once no less alive than the architect who will use it? Years after wood has become what some call dead, it is capable of vitality. Perhaps not in the same way as was Aaron's rod when it burst into leaf, but with no less striking implications. Take down an old table from the attic, where it has stood for decades gathering dust. Dribble on its surface a few drops of lemon oil. It has a familiar odor that serves to awaken the buried past of childhood. Now, using a soft cloth, preferably a fragment of shirt that someone has once worn to work, begin to polish.

Make broad circular strokes, leaning into your labor, delivering all the force of your shoulder and arm to the tabletop. Within minutes you will see the old wood begin to glow under the animating force of your body, lighting up, until what you see rekindled is the life that has lain dormant in the long-dead tree. Each material that goes into the making of something has a characteristic and unique emanation of which the artist must remain cognizant. And each thing, be it wind chimes, fountain or hospital, must take part in the mysterious correspondence between man and the elements. To create, it is necessary to dream; the artist who cannot imagine, cannot prophesy.

Just as a writer surrenders to language, permitting the words to lead his hand across the page, so will stone, brick, wood, glass and marble suggest to the architect the manner in which to use them. To denounce these correspondences between artists and material as mere animism would be to misunderstand. The architect who denies these connections does so at his own risk. The soul of his building will not be visible. He will have become a barbarian.

Say what you will, there are some aspects of life that do not have an artistic solution. Perhaps architecture, as it is applied to a hospital, is not an art at all. Visit a few dozen medical centers around the country, as I have, and you will come away with an impression of sameness, monotony, derivation, rather than of inspiration or originality. Lacking entirely in majesty or the least intimation of the sacred, not one of these hospitals would fulfill the criteria of a future ruin. Perhaps the solution lies not in architecture at all, but in language. That which eludes the architect presents itself to the writer. After all, a hospital is just a building until you listen and hear the slate hooves of dreams galloping across its roof. Perhaps what an architect cannot give a hospital, a writer can.

Not so long ago admission to a hospital was tantamount to a sentence of death. Even the jailhouse, that one at the bottom of the hill, was preferable, for it did not necessarily imply physical suffering and there was always the possibility that you would one day be let out. The fact was that there wasn't too much that could be done for you in a hospital. Mostly it was the therapy of subtraction: Something was taken away from you. After you'd had an amputation, a series of enemas and cathartics and as much bleeding as necessary to placate the resident vampire, you'd had everything the hospital had to offer but the chaplain. And then there *he* was with an ecclesiastical smile etched on his face, exhorting you to make peace with your Maker. The best that could be said of it all was that your suffering would not be prolonged. Those were the good old days, when a single martyrdom was enough. Under present conditions, the hospitalized sinner, rescued from crisis to crisis, is apt to endure enough punishment to *die out of debt* no matter how unrepentant.

Nor did it reassure that the premises were called Mercy Hospital or Memorial Hospital or Misericordia or even Martyr's Hospital, which at least has a certain unvarnished candor. Were I placed in charge of naming hospitals, I would call a moratorium on the letter *M,* a dirge-y sort of letter if ever there was one. Who would not rather go into the Strong Comeback Clinic than into the Strong Memorial? Or the Florida Hall of Bodily Restoration?

Imagine yourself being led into a hospital by firm and loving relatives. To the pain and bleeding by which you have already been separated from the rest of your kind, now add terror. "Don't be silly," says your next of kin. "Of course you're going to get out of here, and before you know it." But you know better. Just look at the place! Not the least sign of a gate leading into a garden with, above, a bay window looking down; no chimney wearing a feather of smoke; no attic with dormers; no dark, cool cellar for exploring. Soon you have been "signed in" and braceleted like a child in danger of being lost, conducted to your room. How pathetic your little suitcase with its shamefaced cargo of pajamas, slippers, your toothbrush. You hold on to it as a refugee would clutch his possessions at a port of embarkation. A nurse enters and asks your name. "What brought you to the hospital?" she wants to know. "I took a taxi," you say in a feeble attempt at graveyard humor. "Roll up your sleeve," she replies. Now you surrender all the measurements that you have always taken for granted: your blood pressure, pulse, temperature, and you satisfy her with your blood and your urine. More to the point, you think, would be to snip a lock of your hair to be given to your family when the time comes. The nurse leaves, but not before ordering you to strip and don the special raiment of the place. You do, then look around the room,

your heart full of longing for the lares and pena-
tes of home, for the familiar roof beams, whose
every notch and nick you have committed to
memory; for the flames in the grate, rising and
falling like voices in a choir; for your afghan,
hand-knitted by a prophetic grandmother, who
knew from the very first pass of her needles that
one day you would take relish in lying beneath
it. The doctor enters, and with that first step, he
makes the room his own. The bed trembles; the
walls worship. For is he not the omnipotent one,
who has come to take you into his wise hands?
His voice is courteous but with an underskin of
granite. *Behave yourself,* it seems to say. Exit the
doctor. Once again you are alone. Your eyes engage the mirror; your chin quivers with restrained tears.

But. And upon that conjunction, I will hang
my hat. *But* there is the indomitable human spirit
that cannot be entirely snuffed. In Auschwitz as
in the Soviet gulag, in the dungeons of Piranesi
as in a room at the hospital, it flickers on. Before
long, you have tested the bed for softness, then
flicked the bed lamp on and off. Next thing you
know, you will have assessed the view from the
window. Perhaps you can see your beloved house
from up here? Within hours you will have be-
friended, if nothing else, a pattern of sunlight on
the window ledge, a water stain on the ceiling
that has the exact shape of Yugoslavia. Even in
the sound of the wind tricking along the outside
of the building, you will hear snatches of a familiar song. With all the force of memory and nostalgia, you will search here for scraps of intimacy.
It is the same impulse that causes a prisoner con-

fined to a dungeon to fall rapt at the play of a sunbeam on the wall or a child sent to his room for an infraction to take comfort in a spider web in the corner where ceiling and wall meet. The process of nesting has begun. It must be one of the most ancient urges of mankind. In so doing, you will people this room with the whole of your remembered past.

Now you have been in the hospital for a week. You have undergone every one of the tests devised by a diabolical science bent upon stripping your body of its carnal mysteries. Surgery has been performed. Your world has shrunk from the room to a single bed. It is a narrow house, hardly larger than your body. Only the strong, capable arms of the nurse can enter this narrowness to bathe or nourish you or dress your wounds. Unable to tend yourself, you are once again a child in its cradle. Still later, if Fate decrees, you will be a small creature in its cocoon. Either you will emerge to life, or you will not. Narcotized, you are only dimly aware of the tiny place, this bed, which nonetheless embraces tenderly its small parcel of humanity. Take heart, little patient, there is reason to feel at home.

Unlike other buildings constructed for public use, a bank, say, which, once erected, holds to its shape through whatever transaction passes hand to hand, a hospital, the moment a patient is bedded in it, becomes an extension of that person. No, a hospital has not the solidity of a bank or a courthouse. A hospital has a heart and lungs. It has a bloodstream; the tide of it flows back and forth along the corridors. Each room expands and contracts in accordance with the breathing of its occupant. The walls palpitate to the rhythm of his heart, while in and out the window fly daydreams and nightmares. It is a dynamism that is transmitted to the hospital by the despair and the yearning of the sick. Who has not experienced the strange, surreal resonance of a hospital room in which a loved one is lying? I have often felt, while fighting in the middle of the night to keep drowning lungs afloat or to stanch a flow of blood, that the room about me was participating in the struggle, how more than once the walls gasped, then stood still at the instant of death. Can this be said of any other structure made of bricks and mortar and prestressed concrete? And how often I have watched a nurse scrub and polish an old beshrivelment until its ribs smiled and the room smiled back in shared pleasure. Little patient, take heart. More than human hands helped make this place.

Time was when every great building owed its existence to some life destroyed. A living person was buried in the wall or foundation. It was done to provide a spirit for the building that would occupy and give it a life of its own, to make a beginning. In the Middle Ages, gargoyles and other ornamentations took on the function of warding off evil spirits that might threaten inhabitants. Long after the practice of immurement was abandoned, it still happens that, during the labor of construction, blood will be shed, a life lost. The hospital differs from those ancient buildings in which living people were immured in that its house spirit enters the premises *after* it has been built and put into use. This spirit is born out of the suffering and death of those

who occupy it. Year after year the building becomes re-created in the form of spirit as the suffering of the sick is set free within its walls.

But what, you ask, has all this to do with the
architecture of a hospital? All these fountains
and wind chimes, the sacredness of brick, the vitality of wood, the house spirits—these are the
fantasies of a mere scribbler who cannot even
read blueprints. And I, in turn, ask: Where is the
architect who, without sacrificing function and
practicality, will think of the hospital as a pregnant woman who suffers the occupancy of a human being who enters, dwells for a time and
ultimately passes forth? Where is the architect
who, from the very moment he begins his design,
will be aware that in each room of his finished
hospital, someone will die? Who, while seated at
his drawing board, will pause to feel upon his naked forearms the chill wind of his mortality? One
day, he too will enter this building, not as its architect but as a supplicant in direst need. If I am
wrong, and such human emotions cannot be expressed in architecture, why then it is time to
surrender the hospital to writers, who will build
it out of words and dreams.

Chapter 5

Quite as often as he was paid in produce, Father was paid in prayers and blessings. Among his nonpaying jobs was that of house doctor at the House of Good Shepherd, a sort of reformatory for "wayward girls" operated by massive nuns, each of whom wore a bunch of keys at her cincture along with the rosary. Like hundreds of other such institutions, it was dedicated to Mary Magdalene, who was said to have been a harlot until she was saved.

"If you ask me," said Father, "that was a bum rap, as there is not a speck of evidence that Mary Magdalene was a prostitute. She was only a poor epileptic woman who was cured by Jesus. At least that's what it says in Luke, Chapter Eight, Verse Two: 'Mary, called Magdalene, from whom seven demons had gone out.'" Given the discrepancies in the Gospels, Father preferred to accept the opinion of the only one written by a member of the medical profession.

"A miracle," I marveled.

"Miracles? Baloney juice! I prefer virtues; they are a lot more reliable."

His idea of doctoring was to treat the symptoms and trust the sickness to become discouraged and go away.

"Most diseases do go away, you know."

"What if they don't?" I asked.

"That's all right too. People are like old paintings. They can be temporarily restored but there comes a time when a patient must be left to die. Besides, people are braver than you think. True good health is the ability to do without it." Doctoring, Father told me on another occasion, was like tending sheep. What you needed to have above all else was sympathy. And never mind that the patients might look pretty much alike; each one was unique, and therefore alone. And lonely.

I sunned myself in the warmth of Father's popularity.

"Everyone in Troy loves you," I told him.

"That is not so. There are those who blame me for their getting sick in the first place and for not getting better. They don't love me. They hate me." But I couldn't imagine anyone hating him. He was the *doctor*.

I can imagine it now, however. In 1986, two years after my retirement, I was made to go to a courtroom for the first time to defend myself against a charge of malpractice.

February 14

It is St. Valentine's Day. For weeks I have been living with the vain hope that the trial would never take place. After a lifetime of placating Fate, she would call it off; she wouldn't have the nerve. But she did, she did. Here is what happened: Eight years ago I performed a cryohemorrhoidectomy upon a woman. Let her be called Marina. It was what some might term minor surgery, but I am well aware that a minor operation is one that is done on someone else. Ever afterward, Marina claimed that she was ill and incapacitated, requiring eight to ten enemas each day. Two years ago she died of causes unrelated to this operation. The lawsuit is being continued by her widower. Marina is dead; I am retired. We are two ghosts to be brought into a courtroom to battle over "money damages." For three days I have slept little, eaten practically nothing and resumed smoking. Would it not be more sensible, I wonder, to delay the trial awhile? The way things are going it would not be too long before Marina and I could sit down together and discuss it in Heaven. Or wherever. Still, I have to hand it to her. She had taken her grievance to seven malpractice lawyers, each of whom had turned it down. Undaunted, Marina had proceeded on her own. In the absence of professional counsel, she became her own lawyer, wrote up all the documents, met the court deadlines. In legal parlance it is called *pro se.* Then, at last, she found a lawyer, hereinafter called Jerome, who agreed with enthusiasm to take her case. Together they would spend all the rest of her life in this pursuit. Such persistence, such stamina, surely ought to be rewarded, you say?

On February 12, a headline across four columns of the front page in the *New Haven Register* read: SURGEON TO FACE KING OF TORTS. It seems that Jerome has put it abroad that a famous malpractice lawyer, Melvin Belli, will be his co-counsel. He will be coming from California to try the case. The rest of the article reports the allegation that I "badly botched" the operation, that since and because of my ministrations the patient had suffered greatly, that I have written "several novels," that the amount of money sought is $2.6 million.

Last night, the author of this article, the newspaper's court reporter, had phoned. Would I care to make a statement? No, I would not. In the absence of a statement, he did what every good reporter should do: He did research. Which meant that he looked back at all previous mention of me in his newspaper. What he found, in addition to several book reviews, was an account of my farewell Grand Rounds upon the occasion of my retirement from surgery. It took place in December 1985 in the amphitheater of the Yale School of Medicine. Wind of that event had reached the press and several state newspapers had sent reporters to cover it. Just prior to Grand Rounds, a young woman, the reporter from the *Register,* had stopped me.

"When does your press conference begin?"

"It is not a press conference," I told her.

"Well, whatever you call it," she said.

"Grand Rounds," I said. And added: "Please, this is a very difficult time for me. It is private. I am saying good-bye to my students and colleagues, doctors and nurses. Please don't stay."

The article she produced had almost nothing to do with what transpired that morning. No single phrase of mine was correctly reported. The young woman had misperceived. "Oh, what's the difference?" I had said to those who had been present and who knew. Ah, but there was to be a difference. For in due course the front-page article was to appear. It had been derived in large part from the earlier piece; thus does falsehood feed upon itself. The next day at the courthouse I told this to the reporter.

"That sort of thing happens," he explained.

"Besides," I said, "Melvin Belli isn't going to come."

"I know," he said. "I phoned him."

"Then why. . . ?"

"We were told he was."

"I have never written a novel," I told him.

"Then what were they?" he asked.

"Where did you get 'badly botched'?"

"From the plaintiff's lawyer."

"Listen," I said. "We are both writers. I have never knowingly injured anyone with a single sentence of mine. Why are you doing this to me?"

"You are H.P.," he said.

"H.P.?"

"High profile," he explained.

"Because I wrote those books?"

"Fame," he told me, "is a two-way street."

"But one must be forgiven for one's fame."

"Feet of clay. . . ." he began.

"Heart of stone," I interrupted. Thus was I educated in the merciful and fair ways of the American press. Each day of the trial the proceedings would be reported prominently in the newspaper.

Day 1

For some weeks I have experienced an-
orexia, insomnia and a sense of bereavement, as
though fifty years later I am once again grieving
for my father. Enough. It is time to go. I shall
attend the trial by myself. The sympathy of others would further unman me. Alone, one becomes reconciled to oneself. Do I have
everything? My notebook, a pencil and oh, yes, a
green stone of polished malachite from Vermont
about the size and shape of a robin's egg. It was
given to me long ago by someone who loved me.
This will keep you safe, she had whispered. In
the absence of faith, superstition will do. For the
seven days of the trial I am never to be without
the little green stone. On the witness stand, faced
with the verbal terrorism of the lawyer or the
persecution of the press, and with my heart leak-
ing courage, I will have only to slip my hand in
my pocket and feel the stone settle into my palm
in order to be steady.

On the street I am stopped by a former patient of mine. She has read the newspaper.

"Don't worry. I'm going to say a novena for
you. I'll ask Saint Therese to help you. If you see
roses, you'll know that she is there."

Roses? But it is February. Still, for the dura-
tion of the trial I will be on the lookout for the
roses of redemption.

The courthouse has a white marble face as
pitiless as it is neutral. Up wide stone steps and
through a revolving door: the municipal odor of
tobacco and urine; spittoons. A uniformed guard
is stationed at the door with a metal detector. He
searches briefcases. I carry only a notebook and

pencil. Still, I am turned back by the detector, which suspects the metal rings of the notebook. I surrender it to the guard and pass through. Before giving the notebook back to me, he riffles the pages.

Courtroom C is without windows, like an operating room or a mausoleum. A place where one is unlikely to see a rose. Straight ahead is the raised platform, the banc where the judge will be enthroned. To his left in a witness box will sit the accused, the plaintiff and each of the witnesses in turn. All along the right wall are three rows of pews for the jury. Opposite the jury are tables at which the lawyers will sit and upon which they will spread their papers. Just beneath the banc, there is a small desk for the court stenographer. At the rear, rows of benches—for myself, the witnesses, whoever wishes to drop in. Already the benches are filling with lawyers, newspaper reporters and townspeople who have come to watch Melvin Belli perform. Their disappointment is palpable when it is learned that he will not be present. Their attention is lowered to me. I do not know any of them. I think of the lords and ladies who attended anatomical dissections at the medical schools of sixteenth-century Italy and France, each carrying at the nose a vinegar-soaked handkerchief. Jerome and Peter, my lawyer, are both big and handsome, each with a full complement of good white teeth. They wear large oxblood wing-tip shoes and dark pinstripe suits. They exude confidence. The widower and I are at the height of our beshrivelment—round-shouldered, gray-faced members of a stunted, avitaminotic race. So we are evenly matched.

"Banc!" It is a loud sharp command from the bailiff. The entire court rises and the judge appears from the wings. With that first step, he makes the courtroom his irrefutable own. And he is splendid. His face is the color of mulligatawny soup. He has full white hair that is cast in motionless waves. The part in it appears to have been made with a scalpel. His nose is fleshy and ridged. There is a pearl stickpin in his pearl-gray silk tie.

It begins. One by one my peers are brought in, sworn and questioned. Peter and Jerome size them up, then either accept them or challenge. The selection of the jury seems to me arbitrary. If it were up to me, I should have picked the first eight. But the lawyers are finicky. The endless churning of their minds! Skin color, a bit of an accent, some peculiarity of diction, the presence of a beard, even their clothes are taken into consideration. During this process the candidates do not look at me, nor will they until the very moment I am placed upon the witness stand. Is it the etiquette of the courtroom? Here is Jerome leaning toward a prospective juror, one foot braced on a step, an elbow resting on his knee. His voice is soft, utterly reassuring.

"Do you believe it is possible for a doctor to lie?"

"Yes."

"Do you believe that a doctor could injure someone, then try to cover it up?"

"Yes."

"If, after it were proved to you that a doctor did do such a thing, would you have any trouble awarding money damages to his victim?"

"No."

"Do you believe doctors are special, privileged people who should be treated differently from you and me?"

Then it is Peter's turn.

Two hours later a recess is called. The corridor of a courthouse is a Casbah seething with plots and counterplots. Plaintiffs and defendants eye each other with cold curiosity. Lawyers whisper in the ears of clients, covering their mouths to foil the errant lip-reader. The faces of the people are indignant, tense, afraid. But here, at least, I am among my colleagues, the other defendants whose trials have been recessed. We loiter in the halls smoking and drinking coffee, and no throng is more forlorn than we, leaning against the walls—we, the alleged child molesters, we who are said not to have paid our alimony, we who may or may not have robbed a gas station. Here too, those of us who insist that we have been battered by our husbands and those of us who absolutely deny it. Someone speaks to me.

"What are you up for?"

"Up?"

"He is a doctor. A case of malpractice."

"Yeah?" A gaze of profound interest. "I had an uncle once . . ." But I have already moved away. My glance happens to meet that of the widower. Unaccountably, he smiles. Of what, I wonder, could he be thinking? Surely it is not the smile of acquaintanceship? Nor is it a gloat. No, I think he means to tell me that there is nothing personal meant by the lawsuit, that none of this has to do with us, not really. I am utterly dashed by this smile.

Day 2

Being on trial is infinitely boring, infinitely interesting. At the moment it is infinitely boring. Jerome has brought a large satchel from which he is holding up one at a time rubber syringes, enema bags, tubes of lubricant.

"This is an enema bag," says Jerome. "Here is the nozzle, the tubing." The jurors eye with controlled distaste all the anguished paraphernalia of spastic colitis. Each article must be labeled and entered as an exhibit. Like a prisoner in a cell, I conjure rainbows in the spider webs where wall and ceiling meet. A woman in a white uniform is called to testify that she had seen Marina give herself from six to ten enemas each day. The courtroom is crowded and as hot as Nebuchadnezzar's oven. I long for a punkah wallah in a loincloth such as those who provide both breeze and entertainment in the courtrooms of India.

We recess for lunch. Outside the courthouse New Haven goes on being New Haven the way a watch keeps running in the pocket of a dead man. People saunter or hurry past on matters of importance. An old man holding a paper bag stands on the green engulfed by pigeons. A woman walks a tiny dog on a leash. Next to the bedlam of the courthouse, the three churches, aspiring in a row, are little models of self-control. The grace of the unaccused, their serene faces—I cannot take my gaze from such beauty. Why should I feel hurt at their cool indifference to my plight when I have walked past them so many times and did not consider theirs? I pull the peak of my cap lower, hoping to go unrecognized. If this does not end soon, I shall surely die of it.

Afternoon. It is the widower's turn on the stand. He is terribly ill at ease. Peter's fierce glare doesn't help. Having been caught in a contradiction, the widower taps his forehead, gives a self-deprecating little smile as if to say: There I go again. A moment later Peter throws him in the air and catches him in his jaws. In spite of myself, I have no rancor toward the man. There is no sense in elevating him to the satanic. Once, even, I think he glanced in my direction as if to ask for help. It is clear that he is in over his head. Never mind. I am next and will do no better. But why in the world is he doing this to himself? Perhaps it is his way of memorializing his wife? Or is it an attempt to keep her alive by continuing her suit? So long as her cause is perpetuated, she is not dead? No, I think, it is the money.

The judge is in a "sultry chafe," one minute berating the lawyers, the next smiling at the jurors. He plays to them shamelessly. In surgery I trained under a clutch of just such mercurial men. I always attributed their ill temper to sexual deprivation. In the middle of the debate, who should spring into my mind but Phryne, the defendant painted by Géricault. Accused of a capital offense, the beautiful young woman, in what was clearly a conflict of interest, had for her lawyer one Hyperides, who was also her lover. When his eloquence failed to convince the judges, Hyperides gave Phryne the signal to take off all of her clothes right then and there. It would not be hyperbole to say that Phryne acquitted herself beautifully.

Later, on the way out of the courthouse:

"Listen, Peter," I say. "If the tide appears to be going against us . . ." And I tell him the story of Phryne. He is not amused.

Day 3

Strange, how at the bailiff's sharp cry "Banc!" the entire court rises to its feet until His Honor will have sat and settled his robes. Strange, how every gaze is fixed upon his halo of bright hair. I, too, am in awe of him. And why shouldn't I be? My grandparents were Russian peasants. Deference is in my blood. Courtesy I had to learn the hard way. This unanimous rising to greet the judge is more deferential than courteous. It is an acceptance of one's inferior position, a salaam at court. Courtesy is composed of half respect and half generosity of spirit. Courtesy is "the civil deed that shows the good heart."

A slim young woman arrives. She sets up a camera on a tripod and sits next to me on the bench. She is a photographer from the newspaper. She has obtained permission from the judge to take pictures in the courtroom. To anyone else she might seem a pretty young girl with a camera, but to me she is a terrorist with a grenade. Or a sorceress who would seize my very *appearance* and hold it up to public ridicule.

"Peter," I say. "I do not want my picture taken."

"The judge has given permission," Peter explains.

"No," I say. "I will not have it."

"But—"

"No," I say. And that is to be that.

"Your Honor." It is Peter addressing the bench. He is apologetic. "My client refuses to have his photograph taken." His Honor mulls this over, turns to me.

"I don't see why not."

"Well I do, and I won't." And we are at an impasse. The judge looks down at a paper on his desk, worries a pencil between his fingers, shakes his beautiful head over the vagaries of human behavior.

"All right," he says at last. His voice is tired. "Young lady," he explains to the photographer, "apparently the doctor does not want you to take his picture." The girl consults a card, looks at me.

"Is that the doctor? But he's the one they want. I was sent to do him."

"No," I say aloud. "Never." The young woman detaches the camera from the tripod and leaves. It is a small win. But a victory I shall have to pay for because now it is I called to the witness stand. And hell hath no fury . . . How I must look sitting up here in this box—like a sad-faced monkey in a cage. And I, who have never stuttered, am stuttering! I simply must try to look more innocent, less like a culprit waiting to be found out. Jerome spends the entire day in a state of outraged disbelief, rather like a professional wrestler who has just been furtively gouged and wants the crowd to know. Is it my imagination or has some of his hair been twisted into horns?

Some of the deathless dialogue:

"Are you asking us to believe"—he makes a gesture to include the jurors and himself in a single fraternity—"that you do not remember at what hour you received that phone call on August 12, 1978?"

"I am asking the jury to believe it."

"To believe what?"

"That I do not remember and so forth. It was eight years ago."

"That, I submit, is a lie." Is memory involuntary or not? I wonder. Ought one to be punished for his forgetfulness? Does torture succeed in getting people to remember things?

And now it is the judge's turn:

"I have had just about enough of you," says His Honor to me. "Be still, and answer the question." I try to think what it was I said to annoy him.

"My client . . ." says Peter. But I feel more like a patient than a client. The word *client* derives from the Latin *cliens,* which refers to a person who is employed by another person to perform some service for him. The word *patient* derives from *patior,* the Latin verb meaning to suffer or endure. Now I know the difference. All right, I admit it, I am afraid. I have begun to credit the jury, judge and lawyers with some mysterious and irresistible power. I am quite sure they know all my faults and misgivings. Doubtless I am wearing all my misdeeds on my sleeve. Whoever said that being in the right makes you fearless? I am no Lochinvar, whose strength is as the strength of ten because his heart is pure.

Day 4

How do I feel? I am preyed upon by dread. And full of smoke and coffee and fatigue. As for sleep, it is a doorway barred to me until the early hours of morning. I begin to wonder whether I have a future with this body of mine. A friend has suggested that I read the "Terrible" sonnets of Gerard Manley Hopkins. It is a mistake. This kind of misery is not eased by reading:

Here! Creep
Wretch, under a comfort serves in a whirlwind: all
Life death does end and each day dies of sleep.

Among today's crowd are two jovial men eating doughnuts, snuffing up the crumbs; a woman with an eager foraging look wielding a notebook and pencil. Another reporter, I assume.

"No," she tells me, "a legal secretary. I'm *thrilled* to be here." Another, a big woman who manages herself over the laps of the doughnut eaters into the middle of the pew, using her bosom and knees for leverage. And the court reporter from the newspaper. All day I shall listen to the hissing of his pencil.

The expert witness for the plaintiff has arrived, a visiting potentate from lands afar. Like me, he is a retired surgeon. But unlike me, he is tall, straight, hawk-nosed and white-haired. His voice is deep and meaty. Immediately having left his mouth, it sinks to the floor and spreads out across the room, drifting among the benches. I can feel its timbre in the soles of my feet. *There* is an instrument of authority, and absolutely trustworthy. But leave it to Peter, who has learned that this expert has been recruited by Jerome from a notorious medico-legal agency in Virginia that procures expert witnesses as a business. Peter knows that the owner of that agency is an ex-convict. Now we hear that the expert witness has never performed a cryohemorrhoidectomy. Has he ever seen one performed? No, it is a procedure developed since his retirement. But, he insists, he has read extensively in the medical literature. He has personally discussed the technique with leaders in the field. He has spoken with Melvin Belli (that one again). His fee for testifying is five thousand dollars per day. In all his years of surgery, he rumbles *andante pomposa*, he has never seen a more blatant case of malpractice. Is he aware that a cryohemorrhoidectomy is an operation that is performed every day and many times a day in this city and elsewhere? If so, he replies, it must not be allowed to go on. If the expert witness cannot be profound, he will be emphatic.

Yet another recess. Justice, I see, is as much a matter of coffee and cigarettes as it is of evidence and debate. My body has an entire repertory of aches and pains. I take it off into a corner, give it a hug of commiseration. The court reporter has discovered me cringing. Despite Peter's strict instructions, we have another conversation.

He: "I admire you a lot. Your writings and all. I've been reading them."

Me: "What?"

He: "As a matter of fact, I've been doing some writing too. Science fiction. I'd like to show it to you sometime. See what you think. After this is all over."

He follows me to the drinking fountain, then to the toilet. Even my peristalsis is newsworthy.

News! Peter informs me that they have come down from $2.6 million to $250,000.

"We've got them on the run," he says.

Oh God! Months ago I agreed to speak at the annual dinner meeting of the New Haven County Medical Society. To my horror, that would be tonight. I walk directly from the courthouse to the Medical Society. Some 150 of my former colleagues press about in sympathy.

"Do you want some company in court?"

"No," I tell them. "I'm better off alone. Sick animal sort of thing." Dinner is a huge slab of red beef. I watch the others tucking in with gusto. The gravy! I excuse myself and go to smoke until they clear the table. Then it is my turn. I tell a funny story, then a sad one, soldier on through the evening. Afterward there are questions.

"How did you get started writing?"

"How are you enjoying your retirement?"

"Do you miss surgery?" It is the only one I can answer.

"Surgery?" I say. "Better to bake bread for your vocation. To sprinkle flour, to knead, your fingers webbed by pliant dough rather than clots of blood, to fill a buttered tin, to bake. And oh! The kindness, the sincerity, the *smell* of bread."

Day 5

I am back on the witness stand. The lawyers have grown testy. So, too, the judge. His principal concern is that no two of us speak at the same time lest the court stenographer be unable to reproduce the proceedings accurately. Each time such a vocal overlap occurs, he barks and shows his hackles. I suppose that his preoccupation is justified but it does away with any of the stirring antiphonal choral music that might arise from spontaneity of argument. I much prefer the rough and tumble of men shouting at each other out of the windows of their cars in hard traffic. All morning I watch the two lawyers flirting their capes, brandishing their rapiers. There is just no holding them down. What have these men done with their private sorrows? Where have they left them in order to come here? Now and then I take out my pocket watch, not so much to see what time it is as to look at a familiar face. For the third time in ten minutes Jerome has accused me of lying; for the third time Peter has leapt up to object. I am having trouble understanding the questions, draw a blank, as though my skull were the only place in nature that does not abhor a vacuum. Jerome has just asked me a question. I ask him to repeat it. While he does, I look down at my hands. All my life my hands have been my most reliable parts. But what is this! In the middle of each palm I see a bunched yellowish nodule of hard tissue rising between the transverse creases and extending in a cord to the base of my fourth finger. For heaven's sake! Dupuytren's Contracture. How is it that I never noticed it before? Or is it. . . ? I shouldn't be a bit surprised, if all it takes is suffering. During recess, I show it to Peter.

"What's that?" he asks.

"The stigmata," I tell him. "I'm getting them. By tomorrow I'll have holes in my forehead." Peter is skeptical, but worried.

"Whatever you do, don't show it to the jury."

The judge has announced a two-hour lunch break. I walk to the library. On display in glass cases are dozens of stones picked up in Babylonia. Each one is carved with mysterious characters in painstaking rows. One imagines all sorts of secret messages in Hittite—of love and murder in high places, declarations of faith, incantations, lamentations, auguries. Come to find out, they are mostly statements of commercial transactions, courtroom testimony to thievery and personal injury. "Duga has taken four sheep and two goats from Wawati and Lanum." Whatever else there might have existed in Babylonia in 2500 B.C. it is the banality that has endured. Only in one glass case, a collection of spells in Sumerian: three against the evil eye; one for quieting children; one for unrequited love, which goes as follows—"May the lady fall at my clamor. Look upon me as if I were a leash! Follow me around like a cat!"; and one more spell to change a bad dream into a pleasant one. I could use that one all right.

From the library to the barbershop. Peter says my hair is too long.

"It doesn't look good to the jury."

"Short," I tell Joe the barber. "Very short."

"Sorry for your troubles," he says.

Day 6

Time to leave for the courthouse. Do I have everything? Notebook, pencil. My stone.

For two hours, Jerome has perspired to undermine my honesty and my competence. Each question is sprayed upon my cheek from a distance of twelve inches.

"What exactly is a hemorrhoid? Do you know? Do you know the difference between an external and an internal hemorrhoid?" From where I sit in the witness box it appears that something other than his necktie has him by the throat. His face is red, his forehead blistered with sweat. Each time he speaks, he throws every one of his fingers at my face.

"Answer yes or no," he says, wetting me down.

"Yes *and* no," I tell him.

"That is no answer!" he yells. "Yes *or* no."

"Yes and no," I say again. This time the judge does not intervene. Jerome is on his own. I see him pause as if to skim off his seething thoughts. He wheels at me.

"Did you or did you not, answer yes or no, write a book called *Confessions of a Knife?*" The word *Confessions* is held in his mouth then rolled out slowly. I am to be tarred by the word. If I have made other confessions in the past, then why not one more? I think for a moment of that small volume of personal reflections and stories having to do with the pain and joy of being a surgeon. All at once I hear a singing from my pocket. Pick me up, chants the little green stone.

"Yes," I answer. "I did write that book."

"And what," asks Jerome, "is the name of that book?"

"Confessions of a Knife."

"No further questions," says Jerome.

Into the rank and sour corridor for yet another recess. You could float up and down on the wave of indignation today. I find myself standing near the widower. There is no longer any point in trying to avoid him. I see that he looks half dead, ashen, with black smudges beneath his eyes. It is a race to see which one of us will die of this first. If the case were to be decided by single combat, today I could probably take him.

I am back on the witness stand. It is Peter's turn.

"Tell us, please, why you became a doctor."

"I object," says Jerome.

"Overruled" from His Honor. For half an hour they joust, each lance splintering on my breast. At the end of which, Peter is still horsed.

"Why did you become a doctor?" He repeats, sending all sorts of messages to the jury by means of body English and inflection.

"Go ahead," he urges me. And so I tell him about Father, who was a general practitioner during the Depression and who died when I was twelve. Since I could no longer find him in the flesh, I would become a doctor and find him through his work.

"And then what?" Each time I would fall still there would be Peter nudging. At 11:45 Jerome calls for a recess. The lawyers have repaired to the judge's chambers. The rest of us scurry out to the Casbah. A strange man winks at me. Could that be the alleged child molester? Or someone who knows something I don't know? At 1:30, Peter emerges, calls me aside, mutters through his fingers.

"They have come down to fifty thousand dollars. How about it?"

"How about what?"

"Jerome has spent four years on this case. He feels it is worth something. He wants to get a little something out of it."

"No," I say. "It is too late." And I prepare

to return to what is as welcome to me as taming was to the shrew. At two o'clock the court is re-convened. Banc! is hollered. We all rise, then sit. The judge speaks to the jurors.

"Ladies and gentlemen, this case has been withdrawn." He thanks them for their time and patience.

"Smile," says Peter. "You won." But I cannot smile. I feel no elation. It took the same amount of time for the whole world to be created as it did to establish my innocence.

On the steps of the courthouse Peter and I shake hands and say good-bye. Can the gates of Hell swing open so lightly? Is it true? Waiting nearby, the reporter from the newspaper. On his face the tiniest snake of a smile.

"Congratulations," he says. "Do you wish to make a statement?" I search all over my mouth for a word or two, but there is none there.

From the courthouse I walk up Church Street to where it flows seamlessly into Whitney Avenue. At this point there is a small triangular park islanded by thoroughfares on its three sides. Even in the spring, when the ornamental quince trees are in bloom, no one sits there. Who would sit in the middle of traffic? Opposite the base of the triangle is a windowless marble building, one of Yale's secret societies. It has a blind, deaf look. I have never seen anyone enter or leave. Together, this abandoned park and this mute tomb constitute a place outside the precincts of law and medicine, outside of time itself. I cross the street, push open the iron gate to this park and sit on one of the benches. It is cold, cold. The exhaust fumes are gathered and caught by the low evergreen shrubs. I cannot stop shivering. All at once, it occurs to me that I do not have to go back to that courtroom. I am free. And bruised. One is not taken down from the cross the same as he was when nailed upon it. For one thing, I have learned that civilization, like the park, is a tiny island in a wild sea. There is always the danger of being engulfed. For another, I know for certain that I am no longer a doctor. The search I began for my father fifty years ago is ended. May he rest in peace.

In the newspaper that night, a small piece on the back page: MALPRACTICE SUIT WITHDRAWN, with the insinuation that money must have been paid. The last rattle of the snake's tail before it slithers off. Of course, innocence is less newsworthy than guilt. It has always been easier to curse than bless.

It is nine months later. The little green stone is back in my desk drawer. Until the next time I need it. Idly I run my fingers over the bunched scars on my palms, the marks I brought back with me from that season in hell, and I feel again for all the world like Noah sitting on the deck of the Ark, Scotch-and-soda in hand, watching the water go down.

Chapter 6

Father's taste in music was decidedly middle-brow. His favorite songs were "Shortnin' Bread," "Shadrach, Meshach and Abednego" and "Mighty Lak' a Rose," each one rendered in black dialect. As for poetry, he favored the work of Robert Service. It took no coaxing for him to launch into a recitation of "On the Wire," which depicts the last suffering and suicide of a soldier impaled on barbed wire in no-man's-land.

> O God, take the sun from the sky!
> It's burning me, scorching me up.
> Water! A pot . . . little cup.

It never failed to reduce Billy and me to tears. Billy was given to acting out these readings and recitations. He was particularly good at a pantomime of Abner Dean in the Bret Harte (another favorite) poem.

... he smiled a kind of sickly smile, and curled up on
   the floor,
And the subsequent proceedings interested him no
   more.

As in music and poetry, Father admired
paintings that ran to what I believe is called *mor-
bidezza,* in which a good deal is rendered in flesh
tones and there is a large component of the sentimental. Two paintings hung in his consulting
room. In one, an androgynous nude, rather
more female than not, was shown bending forward to see her reflection in a marble pool. Her
breasts were scarcely more than pectoral
mounds. Her genitalia were artfully hidden behind the arm braced upon her knee. The other
picture was a reproduction of Lucas Fields's masterpiece *The Doctor:* A pallid child is seen lying in
bed, his arms and legs strewn as in delirium or,
God forbid, death. To the right stand the grief-
stricken parents, the mother weeping, the arm of
the father encircling her shoulders. In a chair at
the left sits the handsome bearded doctor, gazing
at the child in helplessness. Androgyny, narcis-
sism and despair were what hung on the walls of
that consulting room, giving it a claustrophobic,
mournful atmosphere.

For some reason that I have forgotten, Billy
and I were forbidden to hang pictures or posters
in our bedroom. Perhaps it was Mother's convic-
tion that a blank wall is a spur to the imagination.
"There is nothing so civilized as sunlight on a
wall," she remarked. Whatever, the absence of
pictures lent a certain muteness to the premises,
giving assurance that our room would keep the

hundreds of secrets we told each other in it. Perhaps that is why I have remained less responsive to paintings than to pictures made with words. The paintings I do like tell a story and more often than not a horrific one, rather like the poem "On the Wire."

In the spring of 1986, moping over my retirement from medicine, I sent myself off to England, a country where one's peculiarities are less apt to be noticed amid the general eccentricity. At the National Gallery of Art I came upon a painting entitled *The Execution of Lady Jane Grey.* The artist was Paul Delaroche, a Frenchman who lived in the early nineteenth century. The canvas is huge, measuring, the legend stated, 246 × 297 centimeters. It depicts the last moments of the beautiful seventeen-year-old girl who had been thrust upon the throne of England by her father's thirst for power, only to be deposed nine days later and executed. We see her in a room in the Tower of London at the time of her execution. In addition to Jane, four people are present. I have only to close my eyes to see again the nacreous child, wept out, her face puffy with sobbing. Yet no tears. Within the urging furred curve of the confessor's sleeve, and blindfolded, Jane is sinking to her knees. See how she gropes for the block, which stands in its bed of pristine straw. Shame on the oak that flourished toward such a destiny! Surely, this is a game. Surely, she is playing blindman's bluff. But no, there at the left are her two ladies, darker, bawling. And at the right, the headsman leaning on his ax. Handsome, graceful in his stance, much the tallest figure, he looks on. He waits. His face is suffused with tenderness! I see at once that he does not want to do it. It is he who is captured in a moment of reassessment. And I know that, once having chopped here, this man will chop no more, but wipe his meticulous blade clean and shelve it forever.

Years later, within the silence of my study, I cock my ear to listen to those wailing ladies, who have never ceased to wail since the day they were painted, to the soft intimate voice of the confessor—his voice, too, is furred. "Courage, my child," he would be saying. "Soon you will be with Christ in Paradise." Courage! Paradise! What is the cool steady thrill of eternity to a young girl? Duplicitous priest! And there, too, can you hear it? Jane's caught little moan, a hiccough really, a remnant of weeping. And the rustle as the hem of her gown overlaps the cushion and disturbs the wisps of straw. All at once I feel the pulse hammering in the massive solid chest of the axman, solid as the very block itself, hammering as though to burst through his leather vest laced at the front, his own blood racing hers, and *mine,* to the straw.

My other favorite painting is *A Family of Centaurs,* painted in the fifth century B.C. by Zeuxis. I have never seen it, nor has anyone, for it was lost at sea shortly after being completed. The Greek essayist Lucian made brief mention of it, and that is where I came to know of it. This work I have painted on the inside of my eyelids:

The female is shown lying in fresh young grass. One foreleg is flexed, with the hoof drawn under as if to kneel, while the other foreleg is braced to spring up. In one arm she cradles a baby centaur, giving it suck at her human breast; another, its twin, she feeds at one of her horse-teats. The human and horse parts of her flow seamlessly, the one into the other. Above, looms the male. He is huge and muscular with a black mane that falls from his head to cover his back. His chest is swathed in it. Laughing, he holds up a lion's whelp that he has captured, holds it close over their heads to frighten the babies, who press themselves into their mother, never ceasing to suck. Even in the bosom of his family, the male is all wildness and cruel play, a savage of the hills.

Not currently in estrus (she is, after all, lac-tating and therefore not in immediate sexual thrall to her consort), the centauress is reserved until, goaded from the chaste pleasure of breastfeeding by the horseplay of her mate, she stirs. She is not yet at the point of administering reproof, although something about her equipoise suggests that she will move when a limit has been reached. Perhaps at first she was not above being amused by the cringing of her litter; perhaps she, too, is a little afraid of the lion cub. But there is an end to wifely indulgence. A moment later—see the subtle muscling of her back-drawn hind leg, the bright anger that flakes from her haunch—she will have had enough. She will rise and, turning, offer the handsome brute a sharp hoof for his cruelty. See how the oracular meadow stirs. No blade of grass so inert but Zeuxis has set it trembling in her cause.

And will that be all? Will the male, then, give one last threatening swipe with the cub and sen-sibly withdraw? Perhaps. But in the best of fami-lies things have a habit of rollicking out of control. Although not so likely among centaurs as among thoroughbred humans, games can turn murderous. There is temper; there is rage; there is masculine pride. His flank, where she kicked him, hurts. Might he not suddenly hurl the lion cub from him and, unmindful of the cries of her babies, batter the mother with fist and hoof? O see how she lies now upon the grass that is richly enameled with her blood. May he not, his fury fed by her whimpering, turn his mighty tramplers upon his own young?

All this I see when I close my eyes and behold *A Family of Centaurs.* Ah, but you presume too much, you say. Zeuxis meant no cruelty. He meant only to show the beauty and romance of these exotic creatures. That's what *you* say. But if Zeuxis can beget centaurs out of paint and brush, I can make them my own. It is the sublime reciprocity of Art.

Three times a week at seven o'clock in the evening, someone sitting in the balcony of 42 or 46 Second Street might look out and see the door to 45 open and a skinny, oddly dressed boy of perhaps seven, rather small for his age, emerge and descend the six steps of the stoop, holding on to the wrought-iron railing. His destination is the Troy Public Library two blocks away. It is dusk and the street lamp in front of the house has been lit. The boy lifts his gaze and squints against the harsh filament in the bulb. At the corner he looks down at his shadow, reaching out for it as for a companion. If it weren't for the shadow, he might be invisible. An hour later he will return, his arms piled with books. Later, in his bed, he will read far into the night: *The Green Fairy Tale Book, The Blue, The Violet,* Russian fairy tales and Persian, myths of ancient Greece, the fables of Aesop and the Brothers Grimm. His dreams are full of ogres, trolls and trapped princesses, talking fish, roses that bleed. Even while awake he will dream of centaurs and angels and sea nymphs lying on a coral reef, brushing back their cold hair with cold fingers.

Early on, the battle had been drawn between Mother and Father. The prize: my soul. While he wanted me to become a doctor, she was just as determined that I become a poet. Somehow I knew that their mutual resentments had been civilized into this rivalry, that I was the field upon which the battle was to be fought.

Father was uneasy. "Can all that reading of fairy tales be good for a boy?"

"It is part of the formation," she replied.

"Formation of what?"

"Formation of an artist."

"No, he has a surgeon's hands. Both strong and delicate."

"A surgeon! God forbid! He'll be a poet. It is in his eyes. That yonderly look—he seems already to have departed for another world."

"What a lot of nonsense!"

"It is your own egotism at work. Just because kittens are born in an oven does not make them loaves of bread."

I went on reading: the fairy tales of Oscar Wilde, *The Arabian Nights* and *The Chronicles of Pantouflia* by Andrew Lang, whose heroes were Prince Prigio and Prince Ricardo, all that romantic piffle among royalty involving a magic carpet and a princess who could assume any shape. The time came when I could not bear one more enchanted wood full of nymphs and dumb people. Magic, I decided, was all very well but it took the fun out of performing daring feats. On the ceiling of the Children's room at the library there was a green stain of mildew. It had the shape of a woman's head, turned away and with her long hair streaming. It was Eurydice, I decided, back in Hades and out of reach and I was Orpheus hacked to pieces and with all the parts of me singing on. Miss O'Toole was constantly shushing the man whose job it was to wax and polish the floor.

"Ssssshhh! Can't you see that the poor children are reading?" As though we were invalids who must not be disturbed. I begged the librarian to let me out of the children's room. "Not yet," she said, and led me to a shelf containing the stories of Edgar Allan Poe and the novels of Rafael Sabatini.

It was another six months before I had the thrill of being admitted to the adult stacks of the library, three stories of shelves with narrow aisles between and floors of smoked glass through which a spectral greenish light was transmitted. It gave the stacks a strange, subaquarial look. And there I found the *Odyssey* and the *Iliad,* which changed my life forever. Obsessed with Homer's heroes and steeped in the novels of Sabatini, my own life seemed to me to have nothing of the heroic. Puny, ill-clothed so as to resemble an ungainly parcel, distracted, I dreamt of building a raft and sailing it all the way down the Hudson to New York Harbor. It would be in all the newspapers! I would be acclaimed the Admiral of New York! Or I would be like that big Irishman I watched through the window of the Central Tavern, the one who lifted a screaming woman over his head with one hand while drinking a glass of beer. How like a centaur he was, only one step removed, with his thick black hair and bulging neck veins. I think now that Father was partially right about those fairy tales. It is to them that I attribute the state of exalted sentimentality that has persisted throughout a lifetime of scientific study and surgery. I like to think that they are also responsible for a certain state of wonder. Of all the blessings for which I am grateful, primary is that three decades of surgery have not robbed me of my illusions about the human body, for which I continue to share the poet Marianne Moore's awe for a cherry: "What sap went through that little thread to make the cherry red!"

I had only to open a book to drift off into my imagination. I was oblivious to the world. After speaking to me for some minutes and getting no reply, Mother would steal up and deliver the "Indian Love Call" straight into my ear.

"When I'm calling you . . ." and I would come to with a start.

"That is the trouble with hazel eyes," she said. "They are murky. Never seem to be truly there, looking at you but seeing something else. Blue and brown now, like Billy's and your father's, they are of this world."

The war between Father and Mother was hardly a fair fight. While she had only her bewitching voice, he had all the secrets of the medical priesthood. Once, attempting to coax me from a fit of mopery, he drew me between his knees, then gently fit the earpiece of his stethoscope into my ears. Unbuttoning his shirt, he placed the disk over his heart. All at once there was the distant muffled thudding of life itself.

"*Lub-dup*," he said. "*Lub-dup*." I listened and was *touched*. Just so is the hound blooded to the hunt at its master's knee. It was a year later on a house call that he again offered me the stethoscope.

"Would you mind?" he asked the elderly man sitting propped in the bed.

"Well, well," the man said, beaming. "Another doctor, is it? Going to follow in your daddy's footsteps?"

"Wait! Warm it with your breath the way I do," said Father. I huffed at the disk. "All right, now," said Father. For the first time I placed my hand upon a fellow human being in the diagnostic act and heard the wild irregularity of auricular fibrillation that has no logical sequence. Mother could never compete with that. Again and again Father would position me on a stoop where I would hear the outcries of childbirth in a home delivery, or in a parlor where, through the keyhole of a closed door, I would catch a glimpse of the solemnities of healing. Had I loved Mother less than Father, my lot would have been easier, for then I should have felt less compunction about deceiving or disappointing. But I loved them both the same. Still, despite all *his* efforts, I began to live more and more in my books. Words became more alive than people. I grew steadily dreamier, more distracted.

There is something to be said for having an
infidel as your doctor. The people of Troy knew
he would never give up on them. With Father,
whatever happened was never going to be the
will of God, not if he could help it. His persistence extended to the vegetable kingdom as well.
Take the cyclamen plant that he had given
Mother on the day of Billy's birth and which,
against all odds, he had kept alive for thirteen
years. Despite his ministrations, that cyclamen
was the most woebegone member of its race, a
thing at the height of its beshrivelment. Once a
month Father spread newspaper on his examining table and put the spindly plant up for examination. I can see him circling the table to view
his moribund patient from every vantage, bending to coax the few exhausted stalks to hold up
their heads as though resuscitating them with his
breath before taking up his scalpel to amputate
a single brown leaf. On one occasion, we got in
the car and drove up and down the streets until
he saw a pile of fresh horse manure, which I was
dispatched to collect for working into the soil.

"The poor thing is longing for death," said
Mother, "and he won't let it go." At times of crisis he would put the cyclamen under a lamp
overnight. I asked him why.

"You can fool a plant into blooming if you
leave a light on all night."

It was the same with his patients. He was
constitutionally incapable of giving out bad news.
If there was nothing else to do, he would lie just
to see hope blaze up for a moment in a death-
confronted eye. While I have tried not to delude

my patients, I have more than once followed the advice of Emily Dickinson to "tell all the truth but tell it slant." On the rare occasion when a few anemic petals made their grudging appearance on the cyclamen, you'd have thought he had discovered a new element.

"See that?" he'd crow, his cigarette canted toward heaven. "Let that be a lesson to you." Perhaps it was the doctor that could not give up, no matter the absurdity. Perhaps it was the challenge he had set for himself, a game against steep odds. Perhaps it was to spite Mother. Perhaps it was superstition: So long as the plant lived, no harm would come to Billy? What was clear is that he had come to love that cyclamen, which was virtually without leafage and with only the rarest deformed blossom. I have long ago stopped wondering about the infinite forms love can take.

When he died, the plant was not far behind. For weeks, I struggled to keep it alive, but I had not his touch: Worse, my heart wasn't in it.

My preoccupation with books delighted Mother and worried Father. I had even begun to *write* poems, which she encouraged me to read aloud at the dinner table. While she listened with obvious rapture, he chewed and swallowed and said nothing. Despite so much time spent in the vicinity of wounds, I was not to the medical manner born but was at bottom rather faint-stomached. Just perforating a poached egg with a fork and watching the yolk run out made me queasy. Mother took a good deal of reassurance from that. When I was twelve and it appeared to

Father that he might be losing, he committed the supreme act of seduction: He died, certain that I would pursue him through the farthest reaches of the Kingdom of the Dead. It was then and there that I gave myself to medicine the way a monk gives himself to God. Not to have done so would have seemed an act of filial impiety. Since I could not find him in the flesh, I would find him through the work he did. With singleness of purpose I put aside the colored dreams of boyhood and worked my way through high school, college and medical school looking to neither right nor left. When, on the first day of medical school, I stepped into the large vaulted anatomy laboratory, with its skylights and stone floor, with the rows of dissecting tables upon which were arrayed the stately dead, I of all my classmates had the feeling that I was at home, that I had returned to a place where my father had carried me about in his arms. Perhaps I know Father better now than had I lived with him all these years. It is the fellowship of those who labor in the same vineyard.

It was not until I reached the age of forty that I decided to give Mother her due. I picked up a pen and began to write. But by then she had lost interest in the ancient struggle and paid only so much attention as politeness demanded. Once, needing to know what she thought of one of my books, I asked her.

"I certainly hope," she replied, "that you will never write anything about me." And on another occasion:

"Why do you find it necessary to tell so many lies?"

Unlike those fortunate writers with centuries of attachment to a particular land, I come from no long line of storytellers. The two grandparents I knew came from small villages in what used to be White Russia. Once having emigrated, they never looked back. They were not exiles yearning for the scenes of childhood but late settlers intent upon starting a new life. Taciturn by nature and speaking a broken, rudimentary English, they were silent about the past. My parents heard no stories from them; I heard none from my parents. Oddly, despite her insistence that I become a writer, Mother was not a reader. I have no memory of her sitting with a book; nor did she read aloud to us. It was not poetry that she loved; it was the idea of it. It was at the Central Tavern, just around the corner on Federal Street, that I listened to stories.

A great portion of the life of the town took place in the numberless saloons with which it was dotted. These were, for the most part, one-room affairs, with a long bar, half a dozen booths and tables, a kitchen in back of the bar and a toilet at the rear. From a corrugated tin roof hung two asthmatic ceiling fans festooned with strips of flypaper. At the Central every morning Sweeney the bartender would sweep up the previous day's sawdust, soiled with mud, tobacco, spittle, slopped beer and sometimes blood, then take his bucket and cast fresh sawdust onto the floor in whorls as though he were sowing a plowed field. By evening this, too, would be scuffed and kicked about. The sweet-smelling shavings served to disguise the odor of urine and unwashed bodies and gave the tavern the appearance of hygiene. At intervals along the walls were the brass spittoons, without which no tavern could lay claim to the title. No matter where you stood or sat, there was one of these luminous receptacles within lip shot. Father called the place El Cuspidorado. The bar stools were so close together that there was little room for knees. As the evening progressed, these joints grew aggressively territorial, occasionally leading to a shoving match.

The clientele was the same each night—the men and women who lived in the neighborhood rooming houses and for whom the Central was a kind of commons. In addition to the ironworkers, streetwalkers, bums and retirees, there was always one shell-shocked man with a watery blasted look getting wobbly on gin, a defrocked priest and an ex-professor from Rensselaer Polytechnic Institute, who, in summertime, wore a rumpled white linen suit, straw hat and pince-nez with a black Chekhovian ribbon attached. At a table near the door, three morbidly obese ladies reeking of cologne grew more and more high-toned as the evening went on, saying things like "paying one's devoirs" and "in a state of dishabelle." Excitable as flies these ladies were, responding to each bit of masculine blarney with shrieks and gargles of laughter that had a way of veering off into sobs. Whenever the professor played the piano the women sang: "I'll Take You Home Again, Kathleen" or "The Harp That Once Thro' Tara's Halls." To which Sweeney the bartender quipped. "The harp that once . . . and never again."

Sweeney was sandy-whiskered and as genu-
ine as an oak tree, with a face lumpy from having
eaten too many potatoes but with something like
tenderness about the eyes. It was Sweeney's idea
of fun to empty the ashtrays into an embossed
funerary urn he kept on the bar, all the while
making mortuary remarks about "drinking pleasure and swallowing death," none of which had
the least deterrent effect on his clients. Blasphemy was used as an instrument for the enrich-
ment of life.

At the Central, ethnic jokes were rampant.
Somehow no one took anywhere near the offense that such needling would arouse decades
later. Perhaps the gland of sensitivity was not
then hypertrophied? I do not consider it a great
loss that I do not remember a single one of these
jokes. Toward midnight, the talk would turn to
politics or religion. Sweeney had an uncanny way
of knowing when the level of acrimony was about
to turn violent. At precisely the right moment he
would slide a meat-loaf sandwich down the bar
to the worst provoker. "Here," he'd say. "Muffle
yourself with this."

Commiserating over the injustices of the rich
and powerful, he announced one day that "it
ain't the worms that get everything in the end;
it's the snakes."

Sweeney referred to a glass of beer as a
"jar." "Another jar of Genesee, Professor?"

The Central, then, swaggering, cocky, full of
braggatry, where there was always someone who
would smoke a moody pipe with you or share a
heartening mourn. Nowhere else in the years
since have I felt so snugly wrapped.

Every saloon had its resident bard, entrancing as only the Irish can be. At the Central it was Duffy. He had been in the trenches during World War I and returned minus three fingers and one eye. Now and then a piece of the Kaiser's steel would work its way to the surface of his body and Father would have to dig it out.

"It's a wonder he don't clank," said Sweeney. Each evening Duffy could be found hunched on his stool at the bar, wearing his woolen cap and holding a cigarette in the corner of his mouth, taking it out only to swallow a mouthful of Genesee. He seemed made half of tobacco and half of beer and gave off a kind of shiny-cheeked glory that let you know he was put there for no other reason than to charm the human race. It was rumored that before the war he had taught Latin and Greek in a high school in Plattsburgh, and had been cashiered for showing up drunk. After the war he had lived on his army pension, most of which was spent at the Central.

Duffy had an immense repertory of stories, which he told with something like genius. From the opening phrases: "There was a strange old boat used to put in at the pier on River Street, painted black and called *Queen of Belfast*. One old man ran it all by himself. People said he smuggled guns up from New York for Lucky Luciano's crowd. But I don't know about that, considering what happened . . ." Just that much, and you knew the fairies were not far away. And the sheer wickedness of the man! Once having captured his audience, he'd pause, loosen the strings of a pouch of Bull Durham tobacco, tap out a paperful, seal it with a single pass of his tongue, scratch a match and light up, all with deliberate slowness, fending off any exhortation to "get on with it" with a be-patient wave of the hand. At last, his eyes squinched against the smoke, having tidied the loose tobacco from his lip, he'd look about with feigned puzzlement.

"Now where was I?" in that misty peat-bog voice.

"You know right where you was, you old bastard."

"Oh yes, about Old Man MacNamara, that was his name . . ." And on he would lead us until once again the saloon hushed and shrank around him. The general exasperation was aggravated by Duffy's need to rise from his stool and go to the toilet at the rear. This happened with increasing frequency. Father explained it to Sweeney.

"It's his prostate. Every man has one. Looks just like a turkey gizzard and hard as India rubber. You get old and it gets bigger until finally it pinches off your waterworks. Why Duffy has to go so often is because he can't get all his pee out at once, only a little at a time. All the beer he drinks, there's no wonder about that." Sweeney listened to this description of prostatic hypertrophy with utmost gravity.

"All the same," he said finally, "it ain't fair the rest of us have to suffer for it."

Since the clients at the Central were all Father's patients, I was sometimes dispatched there to deliver a bottle of pills, pick up a urine specimen or inform someone that Father wanted to see him right away. Each time, I found reasons to linger and listen to Duffy—the way he entered his stories, moved about inside them, all the while tasting them, feeling the color and smell of his words. It was like listening to Homer, I thought, telling how Achilles stamped back and forth in his tent, how Patroclus received the spear in his breast and toppled. Yes Duffy was like Homer—he was the Bard of Troy.

For months I stood behind Duffy, next to the wall but well within earshot. I don't remember when I understood that he was playing straight to me, that his language had gone from the vernacular to the "highfalutin," as the regulars put it.

One day, he half turned and muttered over his shoulder: "Can't see you back there, Dickie boy. Here, get up on this stool." He dusted it ceremonially with his cap. From then on I sat at the bar like a regular.

Duffy was the easiest thing in the world to get going. You had to prime him just once.

"Ho, Duffy! What's the most awful thing you ever seen?" asked one of the regulars.

"Your puss."

"No, really. What was it?"

"The most awful thing?" There would be the long silence of an empty glass while Duffy rolled a cigarette, lit up and blew out a cloud of smoke and story. Who could say where one left off and the other began? "There was this big black bull lived on a farm over by Wynantskill. I had to pass the pasture twice a day going to and from school. A mean, mean bull—us kids were that scared to go too near the fence. Which didn't keep us from taking up a dare. We'd sit right on the fence, throw pebbles and taunts at the big devil until, riled, he'd come a-loping and off we'd jump, hearts hammering a mile a minute. Walking past one day, I was surprised to see that one of the farmer's horses had managed to knock off the board that bolted the gate between pastures; he had nosed open the gate and stepped inside the kingdom of that bull. It was a fated step. All at once the bull caught wind of the trespasser, came trotting over and gave a snort of outrage. Then he lowered his head and charged. That horse didn't have a chance. Before he could get in motion, the bull had one horn up to the skull in his belly and was shaking his head side to side to slice up the guts. The horse screamed, tried to arch his body so as to get rid of that horn, then toppled and lay on his side, the bull's horn still in his belly, and working. It was a minute or two before the shakes went out of my legs and I could run home. That is the most awful thing I ever saw."

For all his learning, Duffy did not talk down to the crowd at the Central. Instead he italicized a phrase with a pagan wink of his eye, guided his audience with an inflection, a pause, a small signal. If the cigarette wedged in the corner of his mouth canted upward, we were invited to laugh. If downward, solemnity was called for.

Every Monday night the Central offered corned beef and cabbage. Whenever he could, Father would take us there for supper. (Mother declined.) The table nearest the door was always occupied by the fat ladies, whose enjoyment of their food was boundless; they dined with immense delicacy and style.

"Watching fat ladies eat is easier than operating on them," said Father. "It is also a lot more fun." The sensual pleasure they took in their food was contagious. From our booth, Billy and I could not take our gaze from them. Only Duffy, who had no interest in food, was unimpressed and considered them an interruption.

"Will you look at the swilling," he'd mutter and flash a look of disgust.

Duffy was uncomfortable in the presence of women. When the talk at the Central turned to sexual badinage, he fell silent, locked away in obvious unease, as though he were reminded of some old shame or heartbreak.

I saw the likes of the fat ladies many years later in Pittsburgh, where I had gone to teach surgery for a week. It was my last night in that city; the next morning I would leave for home. The French restaurant in the hotel was said to be famous. I would treat myself to a feast. Filet mignon rafted on a dark sea of cabernet sauvignon. I do not agree with those who hate to dine alone in a strange city. I think it the loveliest thing in the world to sit down by myself to the companionship of linen napkins, candles and fresh flowers. Not even the waiter's contempt made the least dent in my happiness. Best of all, I enjoyed a full view of three exceedingly fat ladies at a nearby table. (Father was right: Watching fat women eat is easier than operating on them. And it *is* more fun.) Each of the women was richly swaddled in mauve, pink and blue chiffon. A whole tribe of Bedouins could have tented in that yardage. And the hair of each had been dyed and curled so as to suggest that someone had dumped a barrel of wood shavings over their heads.

What little cries of surprise as they encountered the food on their plates as if by the sheerest accident! How they managed their bosoms and chins among the crystal and cutlery, taking the tiniest mouthfuls! Hours later, they rose, disimpacting themselves from their chairs and flirting their dresses to make sure there was nothing stuck in a crevice. When at last they sailed off with a flourish and a gallant uproar from the waiters, it was as though the restaurant had picked itself up and moved away, leaving the rest of us sitting outdoors. Wouldn't their mothers be surprised to see what maps of Africa their baby girls had grown into? But then again, in my present state of beshrivelment I, too, would be unrecognizable to the mother who bore me with doubtless equally high hopes.

Like many bartenders, Sweeney was a teetotaler. On occasion, his mordant prophecy about drinking booze and swallowing death would be fulfilled. There was the night a commotion broke out. From across the street I saw the tavern door flung open and a pair of berserks come roaring for each other, an Irishman and a French Keebecker, jaws open, foam breaking over their lips, each of them gambling beyond his means. With every punch there was a spatter of blood. They spit their teeth at each other. At last Ireland went down with Quebec astride him and paws locked to his ears. With the rhythm of a man hoeing, Quebec lifted Ireland's head and bashed it again and again on the cobblestones. Down the street another door opened. An aproned woman ran toward them. "Jesus! Mary! Saint Anthony!" she shrieked. In a moment her hands were full of French hair, her nails found eyes. But he was like a lion who had found a carcass. Nothing would frighten him away from it. At last the lummox rolled from his saddle, groping for sight. The woman crouched over the burst eggplant, keening, cradling. She was joined by another woman. Together they raised the heavy wreckage, using their breasts and their breath to hoist the man to his feet. Down the block they lurched, then into a doorway. I ran for Father. A minute later he carried his black bag into a dingy hall that wheezed like an accordion. I waited outside in case he needed me to fetch something from the office. A long time passed before he appeared.

"Eavesdropper," he accused, but gently.

"Is he dead?" I wanted to know.

"No."

"What were they fighting about?"

"I didn't ask. It was none of my business. Whatever it was, Trial by Cobra would have been tidier."

For days, the people talked of nothing else.

It was "the weakness," they said, meaning drink.

"It could have been worse. If they hadn't found each other, they would have gone after their wives."

"The mindless exuberance of brutes," said the professor from RPI.

And Duffy told about the time a feathered dart was pulled out of the corkboard and plunged into a neck. Some grudge about a woman.

"Blood all over the place," said Sweeney. "I never seen so much of it."

"Yes," said Duffy. "Quite a little prickadoo, that was." Then he looked off into the distance, rummaging among his thoughts, muttering.

"By the wound-slit, as by a doorway, life left him in haste, and darkness closed his eyes."

"You mean he died?" I was shocked.

"Only that, and nothing more. Considering the fragility of the human body, it is a bit ridiculous to grow so attached to it. Right, Dickie?" The next day I found the quotation in the *Iliad*. Already, literature and medicine were becoming intertwined.

Outside of the Central, Duffy was strangely shy, monosyllabic. But let him set one foot in that tavern and the malarkey welled up out of him like foam on a glass of Genesee. Only amid the incense of beer and tobacco could his muse sing. And all in a flamboyant, rich language full of metaphor, and allusion. Once, he asked me to read him one of those poems he heard I was writing. He listened intently until I had finished.

"Too dry," he said. "Got to spruce it up, give it some life. The future does not belong to the constipated. I'll show you how." And he began in his storytelling voice: "Used to be, the orchards came right up to the city limits. In April, when the blossoms broke out, you could hear the apple trees singing all through the center of town. Now, you get the idea?" It was from Duffy that I learned that the hunger for imagery goes as deep as the hunger for food. I learned, too, that, in telling a story, suspense, humor and the grotesque were all instruments of illumination. At

ten o'clock on the dot, every night, no matter the
entreaties to stay, no matter the offers of free
beer, Duffy slid from his stool, put the saloon in
his pocket and left for his boarding house.

"I'm on a schedule," he'd say and wink at
Sweeney. No sooner had the door closed behind
him than everything went flat. Walking out into
a drizzling rain without an umbrella or a rain-
coat, he might have been, in another time, one
of those Irish vagabond scholars, half crazy with
literature, dressed in tatters, spewing Latin and
Greek, oblivious to weather, who, when the
money ran dry, traded a story for a pint of stout
or a pouch of tobacco.

By the time I was ten I was sneaking over to
the Central every chance I got, which was every
time Mother's back was turned. Although they
had never spoken, Mother and Duffy had sized
each other up to her distaste and his amusement.

"There's your Troy for you," she muttered
when she caught sight of him on the street. One
night she got after Father.

"You'd better speak to that boy. He goes
over to that saloon to listen to the blowhard,
what's his name, Duffy. Always being Irish at
you, the way he does. It is no fit society for a boy
of ten."

"Oh, Duffy's all right," replied Father. "Besides, between doctoring and storytelling there's
no difference. They're both subcelestial arts. The
angels disdain to perform either one of them."

Here is Duffy on the building of the bridge
from Troy to Watervliet, some forty years before.
It seems that as a youth he had been one of the
crew that sank the big hollow cylinders into the

river. Later they were to be filled with liquid concrete to form the pilings. At the same time, high above, the wooden skeleton of the superstructure was being built. But wait! Let Duffy tell it:

"Now to put up that lattice you had to have contempt for the law of gravity. It was well known that Indians, especially the Mohawks, had absolutely no fear of heights. There we were, the Irish, down below, feet as big and flat as cow-flops, while the Mohawks scrambled in the rigging. The way they leaped from beam to beam, hanging upside down by one leg while pounding nails with a hammer, kneeling in the air to saw a plank to fit. It was amazing! One thing, though—those Mohawks liked their whiskey on the job. No whiskey, no work. And there wasn't a thing you could do about it. Callahan, the foreman, said it made them buoyant. I don't know about that but I do know they couldn't hold it any better than white men and maybe worse.

"I remember the day we were pouring the first of the pilings at the Watervliet end of the bridge. The cylinder was no more than two thirds full of wet concrete when all of a sudden one of the Mohawks, a fellow they called Rainbow from the bright-colored sweatband he wore around his head, gave out a war whoop and jumped from the very top of the bridge. Head over heels he tumbled, howling all the way down until he hit that cylinder of wet concrete. Plop! And sank out of sight. A minute later the surface of the concrete was as smooth and still as if nothing had happened. But I knew it had. When his voice cut off in midyell, at the instant he went under, there was exactly that silence as when someone stops beating a tom-tom. We never got him out. By the time they found a grappling hook the concrete had hardened. We all milled around for an hour, shaking our heads, then went back to pouring. Not much else we could do. Nine months later the Green Island Bridge was opened for traffic. At the ceremony the mayors of Troy and Watervliet each snipped a ribbon at his end and made a speech. Neither one of them brought up the subject."

In the forty years since I heard Duffy tell about it, I have gone back to Troy a hundred times, and I never see the bridge without thinking of that Mohawk Indian holding it up and steady with his skeleton, animating it with his spirit. Last summer I walked across the bridge and paused at the piling that was his tomb. A spiral crack had appeared at the base of it, from which was growing a wild geranium. A dozen tiny red flowers were blooming there in secrecy. I still think they should have named it after him: the Rainbow Bridge.

When I got home from the Central that night I repeated the story.

"That liar!" said Mother.

"How's your mama?" asked Duffy the next day.

"She says you're a liar."

Duffy drew himself up to full height, his face a mask of injured feelings. "We are not a liar," he said. "We are a storyteller."

The men of the neighborhood seemed to me a tragic lot, tragic without being aware of it. Bigots, they were devoid of sensuousness and any contact with the mystical. With mindless regularity they had been savagely beaten by their fathers; with the same unreasoning fury, they beat their own sons. The bruises, black eyes, welts and tight-lipped anger on the faces of the boys at school spoke of a domestic violence far beyond my imagining, which did not go beyond the hairbrush on the mantel. By the time we reached high school, the boys were beating each other, fashioning a society of bullies and victims. "One must be either the hammer or the anvil," said Duffy. "That's Goethe."

"No," said Sweeney, "it's the Eye rish."

By 1936 the Depression seemed everlasting. There had been no work for so long, it seemed as if the men had forgotten how to do it. They lived under bridges like trolls. An army of tramps rode the rails back and forth across the continent. They slept and bathed where they could. In the men's room at the library, there was always someone stripped down and bathing over the small sink. The library responded gently by putting up a sign on the bathroom wall: CASUAL ABLUTIONS ONLY. In some quarters the hobo way of life had taken on a certain bohemian aroma. There was gallantry in flirting with the Dogs of Hell.

Chapter 7

If I have failed to describe Father—his hairless white arms and legs, toothbrush mustache, aluminum hair, hands small and powerful, skin more gray than pink—it is because none of his features did him justice. I should have had to mention wings in order to do that.

Father's professed atheism, far from setting an example, had the opposite effect. From age ten, I developed an attraction toward the bells, incense and statuary of St. Peter's Church. Besides, the New Testament seemed so much more civilized and human than the Old, the gentle Christ more appealing than testy, vengeful Jehovah. I did not see myself or any of my friends among the cast of characters of the Old Testament. Every chance I got, I sneaked into St. Peter's, where I followed the Stations of the Cross with perfervid relish. It had to be done behind Grandpa's back, a trick made easier by the presence of his bilateral cataracts. Furtiveness was a good part of the pleasure. It gave the flavor of vice to churchgoing. Two years later, I renounced religion for good and settled into exclusion from faith, the way one is blackballed from membership in a club that one had never wanted to join. As for the hereafter, oblivion was preferable to Hell. Still, my atheism is far from devout, but a rather lazy, halfhearted form of the creed, tinged with what the French call *la nostalgie de la croyance*. It is that nostalgia for faith that has led me into any number of monasteries and churches to seek out the company of the pious. Nor am I so certain of the inefficacy of prayer, but am beginning to suspect that gazing, listening and contemplating may influence the material universe.

As casual as was Father's attitude toward prostitution, just so lightly did he treat the subject of religion. One faith was no better than any other and, personally, he enjoyed a carefree atheism. He loved poking fun at the hereafter, calling it the Great Perhaps.

"It is said that you don't have to pee in Heaven," he said. "If that's true, the dead are luckier than we are."

Our early theological discussions were terse.

"Was Adam a baby when he was born? Who changed his diaper?"

"Yes, and God."

"Jesus changed Adam's diaper?"

"Go ask your mother."

"What's a soul?" I wanted to know.

"No such thing," he replied.

"Well, supposing there were, what would it be?"

"Oh, a little bag of air, I suppose, like a breeze or a draft or a bit of a gale, only held inside of a bubble. Some of them smell pretty bad from all the wickedness. Others, like yours, smell sweet as flowers."

I put it to Mother.

"What about God?"

"Unlike your father, I do believe in Him," she said vaguely and preferred to let it go at that. When I related this to Father, he snickered.

"Your mother feels the same way about God as she does about Ethiopia. She is reasonably certain He is there." But every so often I caught her praying, offering explanations for her behavior, begging for advice and intercession, all the while excluding Him from knowledge of her misdeeds as though His ears were too innocent and pure for such revelations.

For an atheist, Father seemed to know a good deal about matters of religion. Nor did he hesitate to pass this lore on to us. His favorite book was Foxe's *Book of Martyrs*. He took gruesome delight in reading aloud the details of the torture suffered by the holy. On the subject of martyrdom, which he did not think at all stupid, he allowed that his idea of a martyr was a certain John Ziska. Just before he was to be flayed during the Protestant Reformation, Ziska bequeathed his skin to the Church to be made into a drum. Whenever it would be banged, the faithful would be called to worship. That sort of thing Father always told with a hint of derision. And so it was with no little surprise that one day I watched him hammer a nail in the waiting-room wall, then hang a crucifix on it.

"But we are not Catholic," I reminded him.

"That's right, we're not. But the people who sit in this room are. It will be easier for them to offer up the waiting if they see Him hanging around too."

Years later there was to come the night of my own religious imposture. I was in the midst of surgical training at Yale. An elderly man lay critically ill from complications of the operation I had performed days before. His blood pressure had fallen, his pulse and temperature risen. He was well aware of my vigorous efforts to restore him and, I think, of the despair I could not conceal.

"Doctor," he said, "I'm not going to make it." When I began to remonstrate he lifted a dismissive hand.

"I want to see the priest now," he told me. I left to place the call. Twenty minutes later the priest had not come, and with the man's condition deteriorating, I summoned the priest again. After the third call it became apparent that he would not arrive in time. Once more the man in the bed called weakly for the priest. It was his only desire. And mine as well.

Turning off the light, I stepped from the room into the corridor, reentered and lowered my voice an octave.

"It is Father Cavanaugh, my son. Do you want to make your confession?"

"Thank you, Father. Forgive me for I have

sinned." There followed a breathless whisper scarcely formed into words. I waited for it to stop.

"I forgive you, my son, in the name of the Father, the Son and the Holy Spirit. Amen." Moments later, the man was dead. All at once, the light was flicked on. A nurse bearing a syringe and a tourniquet paused, looked from me to the contents of the bed, then back to me.

"What did you just do?" she said in a voice of granite. But unlike Father with his crucifix, I could not say what or why.

It seems to me now that, despite his oft-announced disbelief, Father was not an atheist at all. For him, as for me, always, the gods have been Greek—Apollo, Aphrodite, Dionysus and the rest. Neither Jehovah nor the Christian God has supplanted them. These days, when the daily manipulation of words upon a page has become a settled, sedentary business, I sometimes gaze out the window of my study and murmur a prayer of thanks or make a propitiatory offering to the inhabitants of Parnassus.

Besides, in Father, the priest and the sensualist existed side by side. His performance of the simplest acts—lighting a fire in the grate, tamping down a cigarette, lathering on shaving cream, trimming his spruce little mustache—partook of these two elements. They were present in his practice of medicine—the way his fingers questioned a pulse. The bodies of his patients were both the pasture upon which his senses grazed and his pastorage. Once, on a house call, he had needed me to hold a man's leg still while he debrided an infected gash. I could not hide my revulsion at the stench, the ugliness of the rotting flesh. He looked up to see the disgust on my face and nodded to himself as though his worst fears had been confirmed. "A wound is like a lamp," he said. "If all the lights in the house went out, you could dress a wound by the light it gives off."

"One day you will learn to love wounds," he said on the way home, "and tumors and festering sores." To him they were among the most beautiful things in the world. I did not then understand how a festering sore could be thought beautiful. I do now, for the vivid colors, odor and shape of such a wound appeal to the sensual mind. And each carries within it the glorious possibility of being healed, offers to the doctor the glorious privilege of healing it. Years later, I would try to write about the beauty of the wound—blood spreading across a pillow, a vase of dead flowers in a sickroom, an amputated leg—rendering the events of the body and illness in the keenest language I could find. If invited to choose one of three chests in which to locate a writer's treasure, I would be like Bassanio in *The Merchant of Venice,* who picked neither the gold nor the silver casket, but the one made of lead, "which rather threaten'st than dost promise aught." It is what comes of having discovered beauty in the most unlikely places. The writer attempts to bridge the wound of childhood with words, knowing all the while that, should the wound heal, he would no longer be a writer. Unlike the wound of the body, the healing of such a wound would kill a writer.

Even Father's smile was presented with ecclesiastical self-awareness, the way he let it break (deliberately, with exactitude) upon his face. It was how I knew that he was unhappy. Happy men forget how their smiles are made.

I remember the precise moment when I learned that Mother and Father no longer loved each other, if ever they had. One night, from my bed, I heard them speaking in low, solemn voices. I crept down the hall to eavesdrop. Through the keyhole of the front room I saw her reclining on the sofa. He stood at the window with his back to her.

"It is something that I cannot help," he was saying. "It has always been there."

"Then why, for God's sake, why, did you marry me?" After that came the muffled sound of weeping. "The waste!" she cried. "The terrible waste."

"No," he said. "You mustn't. There are the boys."

"Freedom," she said then. I heard only the one word.

To which he replied: "Shelter."

I was much older than they were when I, too, learned that life is not freedom; that is a false idea. Life is the desire to shelter.

I could hear nothing more. Once I was back in bed, my legs turned to roots and sank into the mattress. I could not have budged. Only my heart, pierced by an icicle, throbbed painfully on. The next morning at breakfast I searched their faces, but there was no sign. Until his death, they would continue to lie to spare our feelings. In public, they would tease each other with wit and acerbity. The myth of the family would be carried on. I breathed a sigh of relief.

Once given a bouquet of carnations by a patient, Father brought them upstairs and presented them to Mother.

"I hate carnations," she said, making a face. Then, seeing that I was present, she added with a kind of demented logic: "The smell could bring on an attack of sugar diabetes." To which he responded with a small hollow laugh.

From their example I learned that there is no need to clear up misunderstandings. It is mainly by them that one day advances into the next and that people continue to relate to one another. For half a century I plucked at the hem of that mystery until one day an elderly cousin visited and I questioned her.

"Your father was a compulsive womanizer," she told me. "He visited prostitutes. Of the ones that came to see him at his office he was as often the client as the doctor. Your mother suffered greatly from it."

"I don't believe you," I told her.

After a long pause, she replied, "No, of course not, and you shouldn't."

While in all other matters, Father spoke to me as a boy, with affection and jocularity, about doctoring he spoke to me as an adult, with utter seriousness, as though he had divined that there was to be so little time. He told me about those kings who could heal a sore by touching. Almost at once, it would close up and be gone. Doctoring was like that, like trying to be a king. "Someday when you are a man and a doctor, you will know what I mean." When, years later, I studied the art of taking the patient's history and performing a physical examination, it was as though I had been taught these arts as a child. There was a strange familiarity about them that came, I am sure, from watching him at work and from listening to his gentle, murmuring physical diagnosis. There is something deeply moving about the human body waiting to be examined. Lying or seated, the body has surrendered whatever defensive or acquisitive posture it may have had and presents itself in an attitude of supplication. Palpating the abdomen, the doctor may glance up to see the trust that glows deep within the eyes of the patient. Sparks of it will leap forth to ignite him. For it is trust, not gratitude or worship, that animates the physician. To palm a fevered brow, to feel a thin, wavering pulse at the wrist, to draw down a pale lower lid—these simple acts cause a doctor's heart to expand. His own physical condition is altered by the presence of the patient. It is the sublime contagion of the diagnostic embrace. Add to this the possibility of the grace of healing, and there is no human contact more beautiful.

In the process of physical examination, whoever else might be present, the patient and the doctor are alone with each other. No matter how a patient first shows himself to the doctor, it is more diagnostic to watch a man removing his soiled underwear to show you his naked affliction. Still, the daily intercourse with suffering is a burden that grows heavier with age. The doctor will need all of his wit and humor to defend himself from despair.

"So many times," said Father, "there will be nothing you can do except"—and here his face brightened—"to make sympathetic noises in your throat." From this I have learned not to hesitate to make empty gestures in the face of hopelessness. They can be of immense value to the sick and their next of kin.

Everything Father said was a dispatch that would precede me into my life. At intervals, there they would be, waiting for me; I had only to pick each one up and read it in order to find the way to the next message.

When World War II broke out, the shortage of doctors became acute. Father opened a second office in East Greenbush, a village ten miles out of town. He grew haggard.

"You will kill yourself," said Mother. "Then what?"

"It is the sick whose labor is hardest. I am an idler next to them."

"It is all very well to be noble," she began, then lapsed into silence. Evenings, I would go with him to East Greenbush and sit in the waiting room doing my homework and spying on the patients. Sometimes the door to the examining room would come unlatched and swing open. I would see him tilting a face to the light, drawing down a lower eyelid to detect a pallor, his fingers questioning a pulse, then laying an arm back upon the sheet. I would glimpse his thin shoulders, his haggard face and think: How tired he looks, and I would tremble. One evening an elderly feverish man lay on the table, coughing.

"What does he have?" I asked on the ride home.

"Pneumonia and cancer. I won't treat his pneumonia, though. One day soon it will be his best friend." I understood that it would then be time to step back and permit the man to die.

It was in Pittsburgh forty years later that I was making rounds with the house staff in the new trauma unit of a great hospital. The patients were a dozen or so young men and women who had been in automobile accidents, with two exceptions. One was a seventeen-year-old gymnast who had miscalculated a tumble and was quadriplegic.

"How are you?" I asked him.

The boy smiled. "I think I can tell when I have to pee."

"Oh, that's good! Good!"

In the next bed was a young farmer who had been struck on the head by a falling tree. Such an event could have taken place in prehistoric times. His electroencephalograph was flat. There was no hope of his waking up. Every four hours the resident doctors inserted a tube into his lungs to suction away the secretions, feeding misfortune that it might endure.

"At what point," I asked them, "will you stop thinking of pneumonia as an enemy?"

"That is a philosophical question," the resident told me. "I don't deal with them."

"If he were your brother?" The young doctor murmured something and looked down at his shoes.

Mother taught by precept and example, seizing each occasion as it came. I am ten years old. It is a summer night and I am sitting with her at the kitchen table. She is knitting. I am building with infinite patience and care a house out of playing cards. It is already four stories high with any number of apartments and courtyards. From time to time, Mother looks up, turning her face away so as not to blow her breath against my edifice. Through a hole in the screen, a white moth makes straight for the table lamp.

"Oh no!" I say under my breath. Its madly fluttering wings fill me with a sense of impending doom. Mother has stopped knitting and sits riveted, on her face the look of a parent who is helpless to save her child from disaster. When the moth lurches against my house of cards, sends it collapsing, I raise my hand to take revenge. Her restraining hand grips my wrist. Too late. I had struck. The moth is a pale smudge among the ruins.

"Just think," she says, her voice falsely honeyed, "with one swat you have killed a living creature. Bravo!"

"It was just a moth," I say faintly.

"Just! Can you make one, then? A thing so intricate and beautiful? One day, perhaps, you together with someone else will make a human being, but never, never will you make a moth."

"It wrecked my house," I argue.

"It was being a moth," she says with a terrible quietness, "a small creature wanting to come in out of the dark." O fierce and passionate were the women of Troy.

On another occasion she and I were walking on Congress Avenue. We had just come from Manory's ice cream parlor, where we had had sarsaparilla floats. A man was striding along, gesticulating and talking aloud to himself. All at once, he stopped in his tracks and pointed one finger in accusation at a maple tree. His voice rose.

"No!" he shouted. "Goddamnit no! It wasn't like that at all, I tell you." Mother pressed one hand in the small of my back and propelled me firmly along.

"Don't stare," she said, and when I giggled: "Is something funny?"

"He was talking to that tree," I explained.

"Perhaps he has troubles of his own," she said. "Sometimes it helps to talk them out like that." When I had not shown contrition she grasped my arm harshly and drew me close.

"Listen to me, boy, one day you will be walking along the street talking to yourself out of misery, I promise you that. And some very cruel boy will gape at you and laugh." Like most of her prophecies, this one came true.

Back and forth, the Trojan War raged, the prize not the beauteous Helen but my soul.

"Do, re, me, fa, so, la, ti, do," sang Mother. "Vowels carry all the way from the stage to the last row of the balcony. Consonants drop right where you sing them." That's why all the best operas were in Italian, she said. The language dripped with vowels. Arturo Toscanini, she insisted, was the great love of her life.

"The best part of a wound," said Father, "is that it offers you the chance to heal it."

I was seventeen before I got up the nerve to go over to the block of Sixth Avenue between Jacob and Federal. Incense was burned in the brothels then, perhaps to cast an aromatic cloud over the somewhat rancid proceedings. The house I entered smelled exactly like St. Peter's on Sunday morning. Sitting in church, after the swinging of the censer, one would inhale and have thoughts of a distinctly unspiritual nature. It is no wonder the confusion of sex and the sacred among the youth of Troy.

On that first visit, a large bell-shaped woman with buck teeth, creamy and broad, took me in hand.

"Come with me, sweetie," she said in her sharp chiming voice. Then, addressing a man sitting at an old upright piano: "I'm gonna crack him like a whip." When the man threw back his head and roared, I could see his forehead like a dented can and his deep-scored neck, the dirt embedded there.

First, she sat on the bed, pulled me onto her lap and, cooing, rocked me in her arms like a doll. Then she threw me down and cracked me like a whip. From downstairs came the sound of the piano, the man braying:

Mexicali Rose, stop crying,
I'll come back to you some sunny day,
Dry those big brown eyes and smile, dear . . .

When I went to dress, the woman, Cora, pushed me back down on the bed.

"I want to do that," she said. "Let Mommy." Taking my foot, she passed it through a leg hole of my torn underwear. "Now the other," she sang. "Lift up your little keester." Like the child she wanted me to be, I obeyed her until I was dressed and she had taken what she needed. It hadn't been anything like what I had expected, and she wouldn't take my dollar. Still, the next day I bragged to Billy.

"How long did you last?" he wanted to know.

"How do I know?" I was getting huffy.

"Just a lick and a promise," he taunted.

A month later I was on my way back again with all the swagger of the veteran who has earned his stripes. From across the street I saw the professor climbing the steps of the house. He was wearing his pince-nez. I waited until I thought he would not still be in the "waiting room." The parlor was dimly lit by bulbs of low wattage, each hidden behind a shield of opaque seashell. Four women were lounging about, and two men. Brimming with hectic gaiety, the women seemed beautiful and exotic. Whatever their blemishes, they were softened by the bluish smoke from their cigarettes. This time it was a tiny greenish bundle of sticks named Ruby who led me up the stairs. The cubicle was entirely occupied by a bed and a marble-top washstand that held a pitcher and bowl. There were lace curtains on the window and a crucifix on the wall. The only hypocritical object in the room was His loincloth.

With one sensual lift of her thin arms, Ruby reached in to pull a balled-up handkerchief from her bosom and stepped out of her dress. I saw then the disparity in the size of her breasts. The left was absent save for a large dark nipple, like a birthmark. Three vaccination scars gleamed on her arm. Slowly she rolled her stockings down her legs, peeled them from her feet, shook each one out and laid it over the back of her chair.

"A girl has to take care of her things," she said. I had just made it out of my clothes when she gave a soft, flannel cough, then another, and another, which by an obvious act of will she transformed into laughter. I stood by the bed counting her ribs. Another quick movement pulled me down on top of her, pinning me with her arms and legs. At once, her face took on the anesthetized expression of passion. I had seen the same numb eyes in the faces of nuns telling their beads. How she labored at her task, panting. I could not imagine what thoughts roamed around in her head.

But it was too late, for I had seen what lay beneath the brutal caricature of herself she was enacting. I had caught the fatal whiff of illness and despair. Besides, I had just finished reading *Of Human Bondage,* and if she wasn't Mildred, who was she? I struggled to disengage myself from her locked extremities but could not. What strength there was in that scrawny body!

"Let me go," I said. "I don't want to. I've changed my mind."

"What's wrong? Come on! I'll give you a good time!"

"Stop it!" I said. "Please stop! I'll pay you anyway. Let me go."

"You can't go," she whispered fiercely. "Please don't go. She'll think I didn't treat you right. I'll lose my job. Please!" Her grip tightened. In a moment I was going to be sick. *Please!* We said the word into each other's faces. When still she wouldn't release me, I lowered my head and dug the point of my chin into her chest, pressing her sternum the way Billy had taught me until she cried out and fell open like a dead flower.

"You didn't have to get rough," said Ruby, rubbing her chest, her eyes bright with tears. I dressed as quickly as I could, put two dollars on the washstand and made for the door. As I closed it behind me, I saw her sitting naked on the bed, wiping her nose with the back of her hand. For two dollars I had learned just how much cowardice and cruelty I was capable of. I never went to Sixth Avenue again.

But I shall never be rid of her. I see her with particular clarity, her waxen skin, the emaciation, that hypoplastic breast like a dark reproachful eye; once again there is the tentacular grip of her arms and legs, the rolling of her little yellowish belly, our thin chests nailed together, pounding each other with our hearts, the desperate untruth of her laughter, the abyss on the lip of which her body lay panting.

Four decades later, I performed a mastectomy upon a young black woman for cancer.

"She needs your help," I told her husband. "Your understanding." A few months later, he walked out the door for good.

"What happened?" I asked her.

"He said he gonna get him a woman with two tits."

It is a fitting punishment that ever since Ruby the sight of the naked human body has aroused in me as much pity as lust. Father was right. Prostitution was a vice devoid of viciousness. And with something resembling kindness. The ugliness, the stink of hardworking men's bodies did not offend the women. These were simply the conditions of the workplace, just as the smell of burning flesh is to the men at a crematorium. If they strained to create the illusion of sexual fulfillment, it was a kindly deception meant to bolster the masculinity of their clients. Affirmations of masculinity are not to be sneered at. They are the very antithesis of depravity.

Forty years later I came to know one of the women who had been the mainstay of the economy of Troy. It was a girl I had gone to grammar school with. By the time I was in high school, she was working both sides of River Street. Apparently she had seen a notice somewhere and, out of whatever blurt of nostalgia, had written me a letter, or, rather, printed me a letter:

Dear Dickybird,
It's Alice from school 5. Remember? That was as far as I got. I have a canary. His name is Dicky too. Good luck.
Your friend,
Alice Clancy

I found her living alone in a rooming house on Grand Street. A heavy woman in a bathrobe and felt slippers. She was sitting in a deep, ruined overstuffed chair into which she seemed wedged. There was a hot plate in the corner of the room and a bird cage with a canary in it. The toilet was down the hall.

"How are you, Alice?"

"Rotten," she said cheerfully.

"Well, it sure doesn't show."

"Then that's even worse, ain't it?"

"Tell me what's wrong with you."

She pointed to her legs. "Very close veins. Say, you wanna have a look at 'em as long as you're here? You're a doctor, ain't you?" I bent to see.

"Wait!" she said. And began a massive effort to disimpact herself from the chair. Rocking, grunting, puffing, inflating her cheeks and her breasts in the act of levitation.

"Let there be light," she said with a touch of gaiety and pulled the string that turned on the raw bulb. Pleased with the achievement, she set her arms akimbo, winked and waggled her shoulders. When she sank again into the chair it was like an old dog, with a thump and a huff and a cloud of dust. I examined her varicose veins.

"You could do with a pair of elastic stockings," I told her. "I'll bring them over." With the light on, the shadows in the corners of the room were even more menacing. A lengthy silence followed in which I heard the loud peristaltic noises of her bowels, like the lamentations of abused flesh.

"Do you go out sometimes?" I was just talking to talk.

"Indeed I do. Evenings I go down the street to the tavern for a few beers. Genesee, ten cents a glass. Nuthin' like it."

Before I left she took the canary out of its cage onto her finger and baby-talked until it opened its beak and filled the room with song and her eyes grew bright with it. If she was un-happy, Alice did not show it. Never having had hope, she did not suffer its loss. When age and illness had arrived, she had just let herself slip over into the long time of waiting, cherishing her rheumatism and catarrh.

"It's always somethin'," she said.

That evening, I was once again on Grand Street. I saw Alice toil away down the block and go into the saloon. Through the window I saw her sit down at a table at the back. As she walked the length of the bar, she did not look at the men; they did not look at her. Just as well, I thought. If one of them should try to love her, she would surely kill him with the dead weight of her life. For the men of Troy are not strong that way. Without a talent for loving or being loved, a woman is better off with a canary than with one of us. But she could still die of heart-break.

Passion and affliction. It was not the last time I was to encounter them together. The year was 1955. Halfway through the first year of surgical residency, I was drafted into the army. Three days later I was in San Antonio, Texas. Within weeks I was the lieutenant in command of a medical detachment just south of the demilitarized zone in Korea. The detach-ment was made up of several dozen eighteen-year-old American soldiers whose lack of medi-cal sophistication was truly touching. To them, the word *enema* referred to the North Koreans, and a *parasite* was what you wore when you jumped out of a plane. Still, it was our job to provide medical care to the men of the 7th Division Artillery and to offer the same to the refugees and peasants living in the area. The dispensary was a Quonset hut halfway up a steep hillside. A foot-beaten path led down to the unpaved road. Half the Quonset had been set aside for postoperative patients and those too sick to be sent home. The other half was for the clinic. The healthy young American soldiers presented with cuts and bruises, anxiety, chancroid and gonorrhea, in order of frequency. The Koreans brought to us their wounds and their infestations. Long after the fighting had stopped, tribes of bacteria battled one another for possession of their depleted human bodies. To us this was the real Korean War, the war still taking place just beneath the surface of the one that had been fought out in the open for everyone to see. What with tuberculosis, amoebiasis, malaria and worms in the biliary tract, we were busy. In the course of my tour of duty I managed to contract malaria and amoebic dysentery.

Shortly before daybreak the Koreans would begin gathering on the road, waiting to be given entry by the guards. The numbers who climbed the path to the dispensary were daunting. On a day without major surgery or a difficult childbirth, we might see 150 patients. Those who could not be attended had to wait overnight or return the next day. Every little while the passage of a military vehicle would raise a brownish dust so that from the distance the line of sick people took on the cast of a faded sepia tintype. Then the women would hold pieces of cloth over the faces of their babies until the germ-laden dust has settled.

This endless faltering chain of the sick shackled us to an exhausted country far away from home, where we did not want to be. We could not know that, to the patients waiting below, our Quonset hut was like a kite held aloft by hope, a beautiful thing from which they could not take their famished gaze. In the evening we would hunker like Koreans, look down at the Land of the Morning Calm and watch the smoke from cooking fires rise, fuse and drift toward Mongolia.

In just that way a year passed. And then one day, there was Chin-I, coughing and feverish. She was eighteen; I was twenty-six. Three times a week she came to the dispensary for an injection of streptomycin. I do not know how the age-old message was sent and received. Could she one day have heard the drumming of my blood? Had she then lifted her downcast eyes to my face to see what lay coiled and starving upon it? There came that evening when I followed her along the narrow raised paths between flooded rice paddies. It was already dark. All about us, a confusion of stars and fireflies. There was the meaty belching of frogs. In the distance, an ox bellowed. When she took my hand to lead me, it was as though I were holding a pale, swaying lamp . . .

Three decades later, and I am once again in San Antonio. Earlier in the day I had met with several hundred English teachers, read them a story. Afterward, one of them asked, "Why would a surgeon write?"

"To give pain a name," I told her. Now I am in my room at the hotel writing, trying to remember what it was that happened in that village in Korea thirty-one years ago. Oh, the sharp and aching tooth of memory.

Her hut lay at the farthest end of the village of Tongdoochon-ni, where the village stopped being village and became rice paddy. Like the others, the little U-shaped house was made of mud and wooden poles and it wore a dense mane of thatch combed down over the eaves. It looked for all the world like a mushroom. I sat on the narrow ledge that faced an inner courtyard while she unlaced my boots. I remember the trembling of her hands, how she slid open the paper door, the warmth and softness of the floor matting, the absence of any furniture. How we stood together, rattling like bundles of sticks, while the candle stub peopled the room with the shadows of everyone who had ever lived in it. Slowly, painfully, we undressed, helping each other, then sank to the mat. We were sick. She with tuberculosis, I with a resistant malaria. It was more the merging of two fevers than the consummation of passion. When I covered her with my body, it was as much to hold her still as to anchor myself to a bit of the human race. We had far too many ribs; our burning skins stretched tight over them. How she fought not to, then couldn't help it and coughed into my shoulder. And cried, so that I could follow the candle flames rolling down her cheek. How at last, the shaking stopped. All the chaotic wing beats of the guttering flame.

She had no English, I only the several dozen phrases of Korean I had learned in order to speak to the patients: *Ore appumnikka?* Where does it hurt? *Yom yo masayo.* Soon you will feel better. Could such words be the language of love? Aside from that, whimpers were what we made and the soft outcries of small nocturnal beasts fearing to be discovered. Oh yes, this is important: how once, she passed her hand before her face as though to brush aside a web. I remember that. And how toward dawn, she sat up and took my shirt, which she had folded neatly hours before, and unfolded it, then folded it once more, cleaning it again and again with her hands. Is it not from the smallest details that a ray of light may be reflected?

What else? There must be more. . . . The silence of the village broken once during the night by the crunch of footsteps, a man's, I thought, from the weight, approaching, turning into the courtyard, where they stopped. How the silence raged while we lay and waited. Until whoever, *whatever* it had been, had walked slowly away. Three such nights, then never again. Orders had come to dismantle the dispensary and go out on maneuvers. It was to be done immediately. We were away for three weeks. When I returned, she was gone. In the village I inquired but no one knew, only an old woman who laughed behind her hand and said nothing. A month later I was transferred to Japan for convalescence. Day after day I would dispatch my mind across the Sea of Japan to that tiny hooded cottage in Tongdoochon-ni, but it was already beyond retrieval. It had blown out, like the flame of the candle to which she had sent her sick breath and which, in its extinction, had ignited our bodies.

Fifteen years later I wrote a story. In it a young Korean woman comes to the dispensary on the side of the hill. She is in labor. There are complications. She dies. The child lives. But that was only a story. Just a story.

Now it is thirty-one years later. And all that time, not the least word until a month ago . . . a phone call. A man's voice. Her husband. She had seen a television program during which I had been interviewed. No, she could not come to the phone. They are living in Texas, near Austin. I will be in San Antonio in November, I tell him. Could they come?

It is a gray dawn such as might greet a duel or an execution. We have arranged to meet in the lobby of this hotel at eleven o'clock. They will have driven from the small ranch where he breeds racehorses. An hour before, I position myself behind a giant potted ficus tree on the second-story gallery above the well of the lobby. From there I have a sniper's view of the entrance. It is the ugliest lobby I have ever seen, with wall-to-wall carpeting of a shrieking geometric pattern, sculptured concrete walls, fake leather couches, an acreage of glass. There they are! I know them at once—the short bow-legged Korean woman followed by an elderly cowboy. He is dressed in new jeans, boots, a ten-gallon hat, red-and-white-checked shirt with a string tie and a tur-

quoise slider. Later I will realize that I cannot
remember what she wore that day. From my
place of ambush, I spy on them. The man removes his hat. They stand inside the doorway,
waiting to be seen. They have the uncertainty
of refugees just come to their next port of
embarkation. All at once, the woman raises one
hand, passes it across her face as if to brush
something away. For several minutes, I watch
them, gathering evidence. Later, I will feel
shame for my clandestine approach to the past,
while these two have ventured forth in the
open. I descend to greet them. Her first glance
seems to me an instant of repercussion, as after
an impact. When she laughs behind her hand,
I know that it is not from mirth or pleasure.
It's the unfathomable laugh of Korea that I
had never been able to solve. Could this be she
who, dithering with fever. . . ? For a moment
we search each other's faces through bifocal
lenses, her eyes buttoning and unbuttoning
themselves. The man rescues.

"Ahm G.N.," he says. "Ahm mighty pleased
to meet you at last." The voice drawls over his
lips. He is weathered as a gate post, the skin
tanned and wrinkled, the nape of his neck
deeply scored. His eyes are prairie gray, his hand
something made of rope and horn.

"G.N.? What does it stand for?"

"Nuthin'. Just G.N."

"It sounds Korean."

"Well it ain't."

We are sitting at a table in the coffee shop
of the hotel. I am surprised to find the meeting

so difficult. To begin is like pitching a tent in a gale. Once again, it is the man who steadies us, secures the pegs of conversation.

"Well, go on and tell him what you want to tell him," he says, encouraging her with a smile. "You've been thinkin' about it long enough."

And so, the facts. It is always best to get them out of the way. Three years after I left Korea, she met Sergeant Howland—G.N. He was married then. Five years later, divorced, he returned to Korea to find her. They got married, moved to Texas. When they had had no children, Chin-I had gone to Korea, brought back two orphans and raised them on the ranch. She had not been back to Korea in eighteen years. Nor would she again.

"I citizen now," she says.

"What do you do all day?" I ask her.

"I help him." She nods toward her husband.

"Should we have lunch?" I ask. When we have ordered and been served, Chin-I asks about my wife.

"She like cook? She make clothes? What she do?"

"She is a housewife." Chin-I smiles in approval.

"Ah, so she take good care of you." G.N. listens, chews his food softly, slowly. I cannot read his face.

"You wife," Chin-I goes on. "Is she as tall as me?" It is right out of *Antony and Cleopatra*. The Egyptian queen pumping the messenger about Octavia.

"What color her hair? Like me? Or blond?" All at once, G.N. pushes back his chair and stands up.

"Ahm goin' for a walk," he announces.

"We'll all go," I say.

"Nope," he says. I see that they have worked it out beforehand. When he has left, she begins in a toneless voice that is almost a whisper.

"I no forget you. Thirty-one years I never forget. Long time I hope I see you. Then one day I watch TV and oh my goodness! I go call my husband, G.N., you know? He come, he say that's Doc? I tell him yes. Help me, I say. He help me find you."

"He is a good, good man," I say. She nods eagerly, races on.

"We suppose to die, remember? Me and you. But we no die." Her hand, which has been folding and unfolding the napkin, creeps toward mine, pounces. It is no heavier than a moth.

"All time, never stop." Her eyes brighten. Don't, I think. Chin-I bends over my hand, studying my fingernails as though to commit each one of them to memory.

"You speak Korean old times. *Quenchanaio,* you say. *Yom yo hashipsio,* you say. No cry, little girl, you feel better soon. Make me laugh. Remember?" She laughs, recalling it. Reaching beneath her chair, Chin-I brings up a small package and hands it to me.

"But I have nothing to give you," I say. When I hesitate she unwraps the package herself and hands me a small lacquered box, black with inlaid mother-of-pearl.

"Komappsumnidda," I say. "Thank you." And I reach into my pocket for my handkerchief.

"Take it," I say. "It is all I have." I watch her unfold the square of white linen still warm from the heat of my thigh, watch her fold it neatly, folding up her secret, then iron it with the flat of her hand again and again. From the corner of my eye I catch sight of G.N. In the vulgarity of the lobby, he is sitting smoking in a deep fake-leather chair. He has been there all the time.

"There's G.N.," I say.

"G.N. I know," she says. And reaches up one hand as though to brush something, a web from before her eyes.

"I have something to tell you," I say. "I did a bad thing. I killed you in a story. In the story you did die. It was how I got rid of what happened. I am very sorry for that." For a long moment she looks at me. I wonder whether she has understood.

"No matter," she says at last. "Anyway I no die. Happy ending." We walk to where G.N. is sitting. When he stands up, it is as though an old-fashioned razor is being unfolded.

"Good-bye," I say. And slip my hand into his great burry palm.

"Glad ah finally got to meet you, sir," he says. I bend to brush her cheek with mine. In a moment they are passing through the revolving door.

On the plane to New Haven I fell asleep. It was the touching of the wheels on the tarmac that awoke me. Had I dreamt it all? But there in my hand, so tightly held as never to be relinquished, the little lacquered box. I cannot speak for Chin-I, but I suspect that what she came to reclaim in San Antonio that day was a memory of love. For me, it had not been love, alas, only a febrile exaltation. As much malaria as love. But there are moments so much later, when I think that what happened in that village in Korea was something greater than love; it was consolation, a thing born of affliction and by affliction sustained.

Chapter 8

The best part of summer vacation was getting to go with Father on house calls. If it rained I was allowed to sit in the front room, from which I could eavesdrop. So many parlors, each with lace curtains and, on the wall, Jesus showing his sacred red heart, doilies on the arms of the chairs, linoleum on the floor, wax fruit in a bowl, hand-painted little cups and saucers in a glass-front cabinet and, once, on a mantel, a blue-and-white china pot that held the ashes of a husband long dead. In each of these rooms I waited as in an antechamber from which one day I would be conducted into my life. And through the crack in a door, glimpses of shell-shocked men with their stone-deaf expressions and the women who tended them with hot-water bottles and enema bags. And always from the next room, Father's voice rumbling.

In good weather I was left to sit outside on

the stoop and read my book. More often than not it was one of the adventure novels of Rafael Sabatini to which I was addicted—*Captain Blood* or *Scaramouche*. I had read them all many times. Once, through an open window, I heard subdued voices, one of them Father's. All at once, a woman's scream.

"No!" she cried. "No!" There was a world of rage in it, and pain. He's hurting her, I thought. Again came Father's low voice, insisting. I strained to hear his words but could not. Then another bellow, followed by a cascade of sobs. On and on she wept, slowly growing quieter, dying off at last to silence. A little time went by. Father came out the door carrying his black bag, on his face the look of someone who had just returned from the yonder side of the grave.

"That must have hurt," I said. We got into the car. He lit a Lucky Strike.

"It wasn't pain," he told me. "It was sorrow." My heart pounded. Did I dare to ask? Did I want to know? "I had to tell her that her little girl had just died. At first she didn't want to believe me but then she had to. I gave her an injection to make her sleep. What's that you're reading? Here, let me see. Ah, *Scaramouche!*" he said. Blowing smoke out of his nose, he delivered the opening sentence with a flourish. "'He was born with the gift of laughter and a sense that the world was mad.'"

Not long after my retirement from surgery, I received a phone call from someone who announced himself as the director of the rangers' school at Yellowstone National Park. Would I, he wanted to know, come out to teach at the school for a week?

"There must be some mistake," I told him. "I know nothing about the wilderness. My feet have rarely left pavement. I am afraid of snakes."

The man on the phone persisted. "Aren't you the doctor who wrote those books interpreting the events of the human body in literary terms?" I admitted it. "Then you're the one we want." And so it came to pass that in June I found myself in Mammoth Hot Springs, Wyoming.

Each morning I was taken into the wilderness by one of the rangers—a geologist, an ornithologist, an animal specialist. Later, in the evenings, I was to "reinterpret" the park for the students "as though it were a human body." Here follows an entry from my journal of that week.

June 1985

At 8 A.M. Jim Halfpenny appears at the lodge. We set out across the park. He is thirty-eight, weathered, with hooded eyes and straight, black shiny hair that he combs forward into broad sideburns. I think he must be an Indian. No, he says. English, as in *ha'penny*. He is no taller than I—five feet eight inches—perhaps even shorter, but gives the appearance of stature. Reliability makes one taller. As he walks ahead of me, his compact, solid body gives off a dry odor, like that of mice. No, something wilder. This is a body that has scrambled over rocks, bushwacked, forded streams and over its lifetime taken on the look and smell, doubtless the feel, of rock, forest, river, animal. He seems made of bark and leaf and oiled fur. Today we will study tracks and scat.

"Fox," says Jim as he points to a C-shaped print in the earth. "Four toes with nails. The palm pad a single lobe. A loper." We walk on.

"Bear. No space between the toes. They're all cramped in. Hind foot looks human. A heel slows you down. Got to go up and down on it." He demonstrates.

"A rabbit. Indistinct. Hoppers are light on their feet. He's running away from something." Just so does Jim Halfpenny gather evidence, populating the empty wilderness with invisible creatures, divining presences. Each time we pause at a mound of stool, he makes a diagnosis.

"Rabbit. It's dry and round."

"Porcupine . . . a long pellet with a hook at the end."

"White in it? He's been eating bone."

"Blue? The bear's been at the berries." He bends to sniff. "Smells nice and sweet."

"Cat covers it up. Coyote wants you to see it." About feces, Jim is as clinical as a gastroenterologist.

"The diameter of scat is controlled by the circumference of the anus." He says this without the least irony, then kneels to pick something up.

"Ladyslipper," he says, and holds up a tiny lavender flower.

We have been trekking for several hours when, with a hand held out, palm directed backward, one finger shushing, he commands me to halt and be still. Jim points to a gentle slope of grassland from which we are separated by a body of water. The wooden marker names it FLOATING ISLAND LAKE. A misnomer, for there is no island, floating or anchored, and the "lake" is no more than fifty yards across and a like number in length. I should think it more of a pond. But the countryside of Yellowstone is anything but modest.

Directly across the water, arranged in classic pose: an elk, her calf and three coyotes. Two each with a black-tipped tail, black again across the shoulders. The tail of the third coyote has been stripped so that it is little more than bone and ligament, no fur. For a long time the animals stand immobile, as though waiting to begin the performance of a play. All at once, they are touched into motion. One of the coyotes makes a low slink toward the calf. The elk dashes to drive it off. As she does, the coyote with the stripped tail lunges, upending the calf. We see four small hooves waving, an impossibly twisted neck, then nothing but a rumpled brown blanket on the grass. The elk charges the killer. Too late. And stands guard over the body of the calf.

For the next two hours she will career back and forth. First in one direction, then in another, as the coyotes feint and dodge. They are low and silver; I can see through them. Only their jaws are substantial. They will give her no rest, take turns inviting her gallop, swerving out of reach of her hooves just in time. All this while, the calf will show not the least sign of life. Once or twice the elk will bend to sniff the carcass, even give it

a healing lick. But then she must return to fend
them off. Though clearly the calf is dead, she
will not let them have it. Again and again she
interposes herself between fangs and calf, rear-
ing, prancing. Now her mouth is open, her
tongue hangs out; light flakes from her heaving
flanks. She is afire. Her eyes burn with a preter-
natural glare, like those of a war-horse in the
clamor of battle. She tires. But she will not let
them have it! Strange, how in the very heat of
the fight she will bend to rip a mouthful of grass
and chew, so strong is the grazing instinct. That
is, after all, her work. But the body of the calf is
her passion. Has she not yet accepted the fact of
death? Or does she act out of some maternal
frenzy? Whatever, the coyotes are of equal resolve. They will have that calf. And their effort
is shared; they are three. The battle is fought in
absolute silence. None of them cries out, neighs,
growls; nothing, only the thudding of her pistons
of packed cornified epithelium. The tawny coat
of the elk is repeated in the golden grass that
bends and straightens in the wind as though the
earth itself were panting. In the foothills the
sagebrush, frothing. At our feet, the cool, un-
blinking, heartless gaze of the lake.

Now the battle enters the second phase.
Somehow the coyotes know she has reached her
limit. Twice the skinny-tailed dog holds a thigh
in his jaws. Twice the elk repels, dislodges. As
though a bugle has sounded, one of the tricksters
darts toward the calf, asking for pursuit. The elk
obliges and, as she does, the other two seize the
carcass and drag it to within a few feet of a soli-
tary aspen tree in the center of the clearing.

There they relinquish it, once more dodging the mother's hooves. But now there are four against her: the three coyotes and the tree about which she cannot circle and turn with the agility they can. Round and round the aspen, first in one direction, then the other, she runs, flailing.

"Look at that, look at that!" says Jim. "Ring around the rosy."

The sound of human speech is shocking. The coyotes grow bolder; there are whole moments when one has its snout buried in the crumpled brown thing. A great red rip appears in the flank of the carcass. One by one the coyotes dip their muzzles in it, lifting them like Russian flags. And still the mother tries. One coyote turns to nip at her heels, but she is fearless and fights on. A pair of ravens, like black rags, shake into the low branches of the aspen and settle there, lengthening the odds against her. Still this elk says "NO!" And all but spent, she continues to pound the air, the ground, with all her might, wheeling into the saliva that hangs from her lip. Once more she achieves the body of the calf, gives it an exploratory nudge, bends to nuzzle with the ferocity of resuscitation. I wish for her arms, fists, talons. Oh, I think, had she fists and talons, she would keep them from it. It is not any longer the matter of a calf, which I understand is dead. It is she. I am caught up in her mad purpose.

Then all at once, as if a signal has been given, a handkerchief thrown, she knows. And high, nude, sleek, she steps away to the edge of the clearing. The coyotes barge in. In a moment they are deep imbrued in gore. Their tails twitch,

their soft growls of pleasure come across the water. From where she stands apart, the elk turns
to cast a single lingering backward glance, then
slips into the forest. The last of her is her bright
rump, like a small sun. In the tree the ravens
wait their turn. Jim is silent, satisfied. He turns to
see that I am full of her defeat. "You're wrong,
wrong," he says. "That was beautiful. All energy
and grace. To choose sides would be to stop all
nature in its tracks. A calf dies, three coyotes live
another day. There is no good, no bad."

"Yes," I say. "I see." But I do not see. Is pity
a less natural emotion than lust? Or hunger?
Save us all from the "mercy" of the disinterested,
the fair to whom it is all the same—elk or coyote.
The heart knows better.

It is the next day and I return alone to Floating Island Lake. It is calm and quiet. Two ducks
sit up to their gunwales in the water. A coot
preens his wing pits with a long white bill. Then,
well scratched, he quivers once and flat-foots
from a reed jam into the water with the softest,
wettest noise. On the opposite bank, where only
yesterday the battle was fought, it is convalescent,
empty. Or more than empty; a vacancy hovers
there crowded with ghosts. Look! A lone elk and
three transparent coyotes, one with its tail un-
sleeved, circling, darting in. Now the others turn.
Each move begets a responding move. See that
fellow hanging fast to the carcass until he is almost beneath her hooves. How she slathers. In
the lake the ducks rattle their wings, a bullfrog
booms and the yellow-headed blackbird shrieks
his personal complaint.

It was in the parlor in a house on Grand Street that I first watched someone die. The door to the sickroom had not stayed shut. Through the crack I could see the bed and its contents as though framed. Father leaned over the man who labored there. A rosary had been entwined in the fingers, which fumbled with a bit of the blanket. There was his pointed nose, the blue toes, which had escaped the covers. Rapt, I watched the man in the bed—nostrils flared, jaw dropped, head bobbing, the hollows of his neck deepening with each effort to inhale. How he chased his breath until he caught up with it, but only for a moment before it once again broke free and was running away again with quick small steps. Exhausted, he lay as if deciding whether to mount another chase, then all at once his ribs started up from the bed and off he went once more, pumping after his wayward breath.

At last the man sighed and shrugged as if to shake something off, then lay still. Father's fingers descended to close the man's eyes. When he had stopped breathing, so had I. Perhaps it was my own first breath that caused Father to notice my presence.

"Well," he said after a moment. "You have seen what you have seen." And later: "Is there anything you want to ask?"

"The way he breathed," I said.

"It is called Cheyne-Stokes breathing," he said. "When they start that, you know it won't be long. Anything else?" But I could not ask about the blue toes.

"Why does everybody have to die? It isn't fair," I said.

"It is too fair. It's part of being a person. It would be much worse not to." That night, I sat at the dinner table and watched Grandpa perforate a poached egg with a fork. When the yolk ran out, I ran to the bathroom and threw up. Mother raged.

"It is your fault," she told Father. "Taking that child on house calls, showing him the dark side long before his time."

"It is his time. There will not be another."

"And what is that supposed to mean?" But I had come back from the bathroom and Father didn't say.

Just as I am ashamed to cry in public, I should be ashamed to die in view of anyone. It is not so much out of vanity as out of the wish to spare others the hurt of witnessing. I should prefer to emulate wild animals that crawl off to die and are soon eaten by their survivors.

Addicted to books, inhabited by fantasies and immunized by a taste for solitude, I did not suffer the universal boredom of the youth of Troy or the recklessness with which my peers strove to rid themselves of it. Nor, I believe, was it timidity that kept me from standing up to raised fists, but an awareness of the absurdity and pathos of those who, like the two men battling outside the Central Tavern, dared not turn aside wrath. More and more I lived in antiquity. My great regret was that the intimate pronoun *thou* was no longer in use.

Compared to those of my high school classmates, my wild oats were a stunted, wistful crop. Scrawny, nearsighted, all wrist and rib, I spent a good part of adolescence sulking like Achilles in his tent over some real or imagined rebuff by girls. Each of them seemed to me like that maid of ancient Thrace, who burst out laughing when she saw the great stargazer fall into a cistern.

It was the age of brilliantine. No youth longing to enter the amorous lists failed to steep his hair "in weird syrops," in more or less the words of John Keats. That is to say, no youth but I. Unable to bear the feel of cold Vaseline at the back of my neck. I alone abstained. I have always preferred to attribute my lack of success among the girls of Troy to this idiosyncrasy rather than to any lack of personal magnetism.

Billy, of course, with his Barrymore profile, his hair as gold as Longfellow's Edith's and those sapphiric eyes, suffered no such deprivation. Ah, foolish, drowsy love! Would I never partake of it? Then, all at once, there was Emily Jane. Emily Jane, so blond I had trouble seeing her in the sunlight. Her low voice suggested warm cider with cloves in it. Her eyes had the same baffling light as opals. Once, standing beside her at assembly, I bent to sniff the top of her head. The smell made me happy for the rest of the day.

Emily Jane lived across the river in Watervliet, almost directly opposite our house. I took to following her home after school, keeping to the other side of the Green Island Bridge and, I thought, out of sight. She was always accompanied by the same two girls. They never stopped talking or laughing. What, I died to know, were they laughing about? It was October and the cockleburs were on the bushes. To one of these, I had tied a string and to that a tiny piece of paper on which I had written: *I love you backwards and forwards, upside down and inside out. And in ways not yet invented.* Quickening my pace so as to catch up, I crossed the bridge, then threw the loaded burr so as to have it stick to her woolen skirt. With a thumping heart, I waited to see if she had noticed. She hadn't. I turned and ran home, reveling in my coward's anonymity and her puzzlement. A week later, I pulled the same stunt in the corridor of the high school. This note said: *Time: three o'clock Saturday afternoon. Place: the pergola in Frear Park. What for: a kiss.* This message, too, was unsigned. For the next four days, I lived on the *qui vive.* Curiosity would get the best of her. She would be there. She *must.* I had planted the burr on Wednesday. How would I live till Saturday?

"What's eating you?" said Mother.

"He's in love," said Billy.

"You shut up! I am not!" And furious, I threw myself at him, pummeling.

At precisely three o'clock on Saturday, Emily Jane entered the pergola and sat on a stone bench. I stepped from behind a column. I could not read the expression on her face. At last she spoke.

"So you're the one who pulled that stupid trick with the burrs. You little sneak." How I hated, not the *sneak* so much as the *little.* I could tell she was embarrassed and angry at having swallowed my hooks. "Well, now that you've had your fun, I hope you will stop bothering me." She stood and made as if to leave.

"Wait!" I cried. "Don't go!" Just then her shadow, like a black silhouette, fell on the white column of the pergola. Quickly, I bent toward the column and kissed the shadow where I guessed her mouth might be. Emily Jane jumped backward as if to tear her image out of reach and ran away, laughing. By Monday, it was all over school, how the mysterious messages had come (Too funny!) from me, how I had kissed her shadow. Of such derision and shame I shall make no further mention. I tried hating her but it didn't work; I loved her all the more, and spent whole evenings peering across the river toward Watervliet. Then came the day (had I died and gone to Heaven?) she stopped me in the corridor at school and said casually:

"If you still want to, I suppose we *could* go down to Manory's for a soda after school." Three hours later, I slid into the booth next to her. Adam, leaning over the newborn Eve, could not have been more enamored.

"I can see your house from my bedroom," I told her. And blushed at the provocative word.

"Oh really? How do you know which one it is? Unless you've been sneaking again." I inhaled the top of her head and pressed on. Did she, I wondered, know the story of Hero and Leander? She did not. I told her how they lived on opposite banks of the Hellespont, just as she and I were separated by the Hudson River. The two lovers had met at the Festival of Adonis, and to prove his love, Leander vowed to swim across to see her every night. She, for her part, would hold up a lamp to guide his way.

"Hero is the girl?" I nodded. "How wide was the. . . ?"

"Hellespont. A mile and a quarter. I looked it up in my atlas." Emily Jane stared at something out the window. Was she bored?

"Centuries later, Byron—you know 'The Prisoner of Chillon' Byron—swam it in one hour." She *was* bored. I could tell.

"Anyway, night after night Leander swam over to Hero to prove his love for her. One night during a storm, Hero's lamp blew out and Leander lost his way. The next morning Hero looked out to see his body lying on the rocks at the foot of her tower. Whereupon she threw herself down to join him in death." Emily Jane, obviously moved, had turned back and was gazing deep into my eyes.

"Now that's what I call true love," she murmured, her voice gone muzzy with longing. A blush colored her cheek; the tip of her tongue passed slowly across her lower lip; the tiny gold crucifix in the hollow of her throat throbbed. Placing her hands on my cheeks, she drew me down and kissed me lightly and quickly on the mouth. My fate was sealed.

October. The water would be painfully cold. Never mind, I thought. At the foot of Congress Street, I climbed down the bank to water's edge, peeled to my shorts and jumped in. Almost at once, the current began to prevail. Twenty feet out, I was no longer swimming to Watervliet but was being borne downstream toward Albany. Minutes later, shivering, exhausted and with a bellyful of the Hudson, I abandoned the Australian crawl and gave myself up to the ignominy of the back float, gargling aloud the watery ruins of her name. It was the *putt-putt* of the police launch that returned me from my state of sweet melancholy. Fished out, booked at the station house for reckless endangerment and disturbing the peace, I was draped with a blanket labeled RENSSELAER COUNTY JAIL and delivered home in the prowl car. From start to finish, the escapade had lasted less than one hour.

"If you do it again," said Mother, "I shall lie down and turn my face to the wall." The next day it was all over town. Emily Jane, far from having been flattered by my act of reckless endangerment, sent word that she was "mortified." The end came at Manory's ice cream parlor, to which I had inveigled her after school.

Oh, the sharp and aching tooth of memory: Outside Manory's the rain is coming down in sheets. In the midst of the gray downpour a vivid splash of orange as a policeman in a rain cape walks by. A boy and a girl are reading the menu over the counter. The boy is sixteen, the girl a bit younger. He is thin, all wrist and rib and Adam's apple. He wears horn-rimmed glasses that threaten to slip from the end of his nose. Every so often he must push them up with one finger. He is everywhere rumpled, frayed and scuffed. The girl has straight yellow hair and is dressed in the uniform of the day—skirt, sweater, loafers and bobby socks. The boy reaches into his pocket, scoops out coins, counts them thoughtfully.

"Do you want a hamburger?" She does not reply. "I have enough money," he assures her. "Have whatever you want." The girl tosses her hair no. "What, then?" She points to a cinnamon bun. "Coffee?" She nods. Then, to the counterman: "Two cups of coffee and a cinnamon bun."

With one hand the boy carries the tray to a booth by a window. With the other, he guides her gently. He takes the seat opposite her, leans toward her, his eyes darting about her face. She pushes up the sleeves of her sweater, lifts a hand to gather her hair to one side of her neck. He watches in silence as she bares her teeth, presses them into the cinnamon bun.

"I can't eat with you watching me like that," she says. He takes a sip of coffee, tries not to look, but in a moment he is once again eating her with his eyes. She is looking out the window. The orange cape floats by the streaming window again. When she has eaten most of the bun, she pushes the plate away. He takes her hand, raises it toward his lips. For a moment she submits, then sighs with exasperation and finds a reason in her hair to withdraw.

"Look," she says. "I've tried to make it clear . . ."

"But why?" His eyes are too bright, his chin trembling. "I love you," he whispers. The girl is obviously annoyed.

"Look," she says again, clears her throat. "If you want to know, I set this whole thing up, to pay you back for the trick with the burrs. And because everyone at school thinks it's funny and wanted me to keep on with it. Just for laughs. But it isn't funny anymore. So for God's sake stop pestering me."

Abruptly, she stands and goes to the door. A moment later he sees her running across the street. With great deliberation, he takes up the rest of her cinnamon bun, eats it, wets his finger in his mouth to pick up the last crumb, then turns her cup so that his mouth will cover the stain of hers, and drains it. Outside, it is still raining. The cobblestones are the blistered faces of old men yelling.

When I saw her a week later, she was on the way to church, a vision in white gauze with a matching bow in her hair. And with that remote expression that announced she was saving herself for better things. How could I have blundered? One sane look should have informed me: Girls like that do not go out with boys like me. In the years to come I was to become familiar with that air of self-esteem from any number of other exemplars.

Chapter 9

One Thursday in April (I would be thirteen in two months) Father collapsed in his consultation room. There were four men in the ambulance from St. Mary's. They carried the stretcher with their free arms held straight out, not because he was heavy, I thought, but to hold back the darkness. In the backyard the lilac was blooming. Overhead the sky was full of grand gestures. At the hospital I peered through the plastic oxygen tent, willing him to breathe, disputing with death over the rich red fruit that was his heart. Another! Come on! Another! And watched the gray face swivel, the squadron of ribs battle on, his blue lips sipping air. Not nearly enough. For a day and a half Death squatted on the side rail of the bed, then lunged. Father gave one lurch and died. When the moment came, there was such a silence as when an arrow passes through the upraised throat of the regimental trumpeter. It was broken by Mother.

"Our daddy is no more," she said in that formal way she had. "Perhaps you will wish to kiss him." And into that cold tent first Billy, then I, dove, as though to the bottom of a river, and found his mouth, still moist from that last breath. It was the world's truest moment. Two of the Sisters of Charity moved quickly to remove the oxygen tent, smooth the sheets. From the doorway, a last glance at the bed. It was like a frosted field from which the birds have just flown. That was the moment I stopped praying for good. Every time you pray for something not to happen, you violate a destiny. It is no use descending to Hades to bring someone back. It didn't work for Orpheus and it never would for me.

On the way home, I remembered that other death I had witnessed, the old man with his ten blue toes, the stillness. Why do we have to die? I had asked Father that day. He reminded me of the beautiful goddess Calypso, who fell in love with Odysseus. She offered him immortality and love in a charming cave if he would stay with her.

"He was right to turn it down," said Father. "Better to leave as one leaves the mother's womb, gets born and grows up to face death. To stay would be to give up being a man." But I didn't believe a word of that.

The next day Billy and I went down to the river. Wherever we stood, the river halted and its banks went moving on. Up and down went the barges, each laden with its cargo of sorrow. At last we returned home.

"Where have you been?" said Mother. "Take a bath and put on your suits and ties. Then come downstairs. There will be callers." In the bedroom mirror, the glassy frolic of tears on lashes.

I thought of her weeping for Uncle Herman. *Don't cry,* I commanded my reflection. *Whatever happens, don't.*

"What if she starts to cry?" I asked Billy.

"She won't," he said. "You'll see. It isn't the same."

In the waiting room, where Father was laid out between two tall floor lamps with red bulbs, the air was heavy with a sweetish odor that emanated from the casket. It was a perfume of no flower that I recognized. I decided that it was the odor of sanctity, which is given off, I had read, by the corpses of the incorrupt. I was to smell it years later in the anatomy laboratory of the medical college. By then, sanctity had been reduced to formaldehyde. The front door had been left open so that the Trojans could file in. At around six o'clock the visitors began arriving. Dozens of his patients, the warden of the county jail, the McGucken sisters horribly subdued, the Sisters of Charity from St. Mary's.

"Your father is in Heaven," said Sister Michael. I said nothing. Were all the archangels of Heaven to have assembled to reassure me, I should have waved them off as clumsy perjurers. Just behind the nuns a pair of whores stubbed their cigarettes on the sidewalk and stepped demurely in. Then there was Duffy, his breath smoking of beer.

"Madame," he said, giving it to her in French. "I am sorry for your troubles."

"Very kind," she murmured. "The doctor was fond of you." At the door he turned and beckoned me with his head. I followed him out into the street.

"You, Dickie boy," he said softly. "You come

on over to the Central as soon as you can get away. I'll give you glad tidings." Just then, a tear rolled out of the empty socket and down his cheek. A tear so bright I could have read by the light reflected from it.

The autopsy showed little twigs of clot diabolically placed and a ruptured chorda tendinea. But it did not show the real cause of his death—that life had sunk so deeply into him that it simply could not come back out again. Nor did it reveal the cluster of whispers in the hollow of his right ear that might have told the painful secrets he kept; nor the echoes in his brain of the cries and moans of ten thousand sick Trojans; nor the whole beloved town moving slowly across his retina. Autopsies tell only the facts, never the truth.

Walk into a morgue where an autopsy is already in progress. Step up to the slab upon which a human body lies. You see that the chest has been opened, the sternum and its attached ribs having been sawed away. Within minutes the pathologist has opened the pericardial sac, then divided the great arteries and veins to which the heart is attached. Now you may reach in and lift out the heart. Heft it in your hand. It has the weight of a good-sized tomato, and so precisely fits the palm as to suggest that it was originally intended to sit there and that only on second thought did the Maker decide to hang it within a cage of ribs, perhaps to free the hand for playing the violin.

Now take up a long knife and cut the heart so that there is an anterior and posterior half, leaving the two attached clamlike at the apex. On first bisecting a human heart, you will find a muscular pouch filled with blood. Wash it out under a faucet of cold water until the yellowish endocardium is clean. Now see that it is many-chambered, if four be many in an organ the size of a fist. The propulsive chamber on the left has a thick muscular wall, as you would expect, since it has to service the farthest toe with blood. The ventricle on the right, having only the nearby lungs to supply, needs no such brute force and is suitably thinner-walled. The two auricles receive the blood returning to the heart. The lining of each ventricle is thrown into folds or trabeculations that would seem to be organic responses to the jet and turbulence of the blood. The upper portions of these chambers are strung with a lacery of fine fibrous chords that go from the muscle of the heart to the cusps of the valves, holding them in place like tent ropes. These chorda tendinea have none of the brawn of the ventricles but are delicate strings that seem made for the blood to fret upon. And they are indeed fragile. For it happens that one of these chordae will rupture, tearing loose from one of its attachments so that the lax strand washes back and forth in the stream. Then the leaflet of the valve is no longer held in place but flaps and billows like a tent whose pegs have come unmoored. A portion of the blood thrust out from the heart is regurgitated back through the unclosed gate and the heart fails. Even as the violin, one of whose strings has broken, cannot fulfill its potential, so too is the heart with a lost chord left hampered and lame, and never so easy as a violin to be re-strung.

When all the visitors had gone, Mother stood between us before the casket in the waiting room for a last look at the unbearable. After moments of silence in which I dared not breathe, she disengaged her hands from ours and reached up to push a cruel hairpin deep into her hair.

"You do not belong to me anymore," she announced. "You are men." Just so, with her tragic flair had she changed the waiting room into a theater. When at last I dared to look at Billy, his face bore the stunned look of someone who had been slapped. It was not our grief then that would concern her. Together, we two men stepped from that room into the endless convalescence of bereavement. In the distance a freight train was buffeting along. In a few minutes, when it crossed Fifth Avenue, the windows of the house would rattle.

Weeks of grief and fatigue, that gray-faced thing. The freight trains no longer deepened sleep, but each boxcar was a pain that Troy was glad to get rid of.

The summer passed, September, October. If only it would snow. Perhaps then . . . At last, on the first of November, a heavy fall returned the old soot bag to a state of virginity. And with it the black furry beast lumbered off my chest. I made plans. Now I *would* get out of this town, away from these trees with their branches knotted with dead nests, out of this damned city, where every street corner was just another place to die. I would hop the Montrealer going north and never come back.

"You're too thin," said Mother. "Look at you, like a candle in a draft. I'll make you some oatmeal." Yes, oatmeal. Instead I went over to the Central, to Duffy.

"Stop looking at me like that," I told him. What I didn't know was that Mother and he had had a talk. He wasn't entirely mine anymore.

"Well, what about it?" he asked.

"What about what?"

"Come on, Dickie boy. There's no sense farting against the thunder."

"That is stupid," I blurted out. I had had enough of unmasking the lies of my elders. At thirteen I was dog tired. "Tell us about Aeneas," I said, "how he escaped from the burning city carrying his old daddy, Anchises, on his back."

Duffy rolled a cigarette and handed it to me. By then I was already punctuating my life with them.

"The *Iliad* again? Forget it. It's just another catalog of woes. Where are you planning to go?"

"My business," I said. "Give me a sip of your beer."

"The hell I will. I'd pour it on the floor first."

"Buffoon!" I shouted. "Liar!" and ran out the door.

A month later I went back to the saloon. Duffy motioned me over to the stool next to his.

"A Moxie for the young master!" he called out to Sweeney. "Been waiting for you," he said. Then he just started in as if nothing had happened. "You know, about a morning's walk north of Cohoes there used to be an old settlement called Pity Me. No more than a dozen vine-clad cottages. I went there once as a boy. About your age. It's all gone now, disappeared from the face of the earth one night, not a stick left. Folks said that in October that year the river turned thick and dark as blood. Well, not really blood, but the next thing to it—the sister of blood." On and on he spun, in his voice that was like the river, his only eye never more terribly blue, until slowly my spirits began to rise like dough after the kneading and my heart stopped aching. I would stay in Troy.

All through high school I frequented the Central. Home from college I went to the Central. The day before I entered medical school, I went to see Duffy.

"I won't be coming around for a while," I said, and told him why.

"You'd better hurry up about it," said Duffy. "All this metal floating around my bones. Nobody else going to dig it out of Duffy. Nobody but you. Here, feel." He took my index finger and rolled it over his arm. I felt the hard scar that encased the metallic foreign body.

"Save that one for me," I told him. "I'll keep it for a relic." But I never did get to do it. In my second year at medical school, Duffy, in the middle of a story, paused, gave that be-patient wave of the hand and slid from his bar stool, dead. So far as anyone knew, there was no next of kin. I was his only heir. My legacy—storytelling.

Twelve miles away, at Union College, I read French Romantic poetry, the odes of Horace and Catullus and nineteenth-century American fiction. I dissected a cat and a fetal pig and played the alchemist in quantitative and qualitative chemistry. Of these, I remember only the day a sparrow flew into the laboratory, circled the room twice and expired from the fumes of hydrogen sulfide. When the time came to apply to medical school, I went to the professor of biology.

"I wouldn't if I were you," he advised. "You're not what they want." It was advice I chose not to take.

"You are quite mistaken," I told him. "It is my destiny." At the interview in Albany, the dean perused my dossier in silence, then toyed with his pencil.

"Why do you want to go to medical school?" he asked, stifling a yawn.

"Because I want to dissect a human body. I want to see where everything lies, what the parts look like. Then I want to find out how they work and what can go wrong with them and how to repair them."

"And after that?"

"After that, I'll think again."

"And why Albany Medical College?"

"I want to be near my mother in case she has need of me."

"A mama's boy, are you?"

"Yes. I am. *My* mama's boy for all time."

The dean was a large man who had once been fleshy but whose face and neck were hung with an elaborate drapery of loose skin. I could have grabbed his face up by the handful, like a bulldog. For a long moment, the dewlap waggled, then was still.

"Another thing," I said. "I only have enough money for one year. After that, I shall have to work."

"And what if we do not accept you?"

"Then I will go to the ends of the earth," I told him, "until someone does."

"Who is your favorite poet?"

"Emily Dickinson."

"Why is that?"

"Because she told the whole horrible truth about the human body."

"That will be all," he said. The next day, I received word that I had been accepted. Four years later, at a party after my commencement, the dean called me aside.

"Well, mama's boy, I see that you have made it. I'm a mama's boy too, only I never admitted it to myself until the day I interviewed you. I want to thank you for that."

I think now that, thanks to Duffy, I became a storyteller. I remember, as a resident in surgery at Yale, rushing home whenever I could to my family. My boys were six and five years old. All through supper and their bath, I took pains to set the stage for what was to come—the nightly story with which I would terrify and elate them—dropping tantalizing hints of the plot, and by suggestion and innuendo generally whipping them into a frenzy of anticipation. Once I had them in bed, I would turn off the light, touch a match to a ceremonial candle, and transform that bedroom into the boudoir of Scheherazade. Oh, not in this reedy little voice in which I now speak, but in a rich, meaty baritone that, once having left my lips, sank to the floor and spread out across the room, causing the bed itself to vibrate with nameless dread.

"Once upon a time," I began, "there were two little boys, about your age, I suppose, who lived in a village called Pity Me on the edge of a dark, dark forest." In the bed, four pupils dilated as one. There followed a fearsome encounter with a monster, the long anguish of capture, sadistically drawn-out suspense and, at the end, a last-minute rescue. Midway through my recitation, there they would be huddled together, their skinny arms and legs wrapped about one another. The moment came when they could bear it no longer.

"Stop! Stop!" they cried. "No more!"

"All right, then, I'll stop there." And stop I did, only to hear a moment later, as I knew I would: "More! More! Don't stop!" And so with feigned reluctance, I would resume my nightmarish tale, leading the two wretched creatures through Africas of terror, full of phantoms, and with blood dripping from the trees. (What in God's name had died up there?) And all punctuated by groans and deep sighs of damnation and mad laughter. I was particularly good at mad laughter. Another member of the household said it was a form of child molestation for which I ought to be arrested.

Years later, when I began to write, I was to use humor and the grotesque as instruments of illumination. But now the humor was not so much in the subject as it was couched in the language itself, and now, as then, nothing is too horrible for me to contemplate. (It is the surgeon in me. Surgeons love horror, don't you know?)

In the months that followed Father's death I sometimes saw him on the street. It was always the same: he was wearing his long overcoat and the fedora, and he was walking briskly away. He was not dead! It was all a mistake! And I would run to catch up with him, calling out: Father! Father! And even reaching for his hand. Each time, when the man turned, and I saw that it was not . . . no, it was not he, there was that fresh wave of desolation.

One year after Father died, I was sitting in the balcony of Proctor's Theatre, where on Saturday afternoon for twenty cents you could see a double feature and a vaudeville show. On the screen Jeanette MacDonald had taken umbrage at something Nelson Eddy had done. At last, the misunderstanding having been cleared up, she yielded to his blandishments. Then came the vaudeville, a shabby affair consisting of four dogs wearing tuxedos and ball gowns and dancing the minuet—step, turn, bow—followed by a family of acrobats and sundry other performers. I remember the fire-eater, a woebegone thin man who, despite his calling, had not the least spark about him. He it was who lit the end of a torch, then thrust it into his mouth again and again, swallowing flame, bolus upon bolus of it, as if to slake a dark cold parch. I remember too an elderly shawled singer, the smallness of her, her face scored by grief. Hobbling to center stage, she waited for the piano introduction and sang in a husky beer-garden voice.

I didn't raise my boy to be a soldier,
I brought him up to be my pride and joy.
Who dares to lay a musket on his shoulder
To shoot some other mother's darling
    boy?

Now it was Jeanette again in the second feature. Fickle Jeanette being courted by a different man this time, a handsome tenor. Once again, she has turned petulant. They are in a public garden near a pond with waterfowl. In his eagerness to impress her, the tenor had become reckless with one of the geese and sustained a nip on the finger. In obviously great pain, he holds up his finger, singing "I Want Sympathy," but testy Jeanette remains unmoved. Rapt, I did not at first notice that the seat next to mine had become occupied. Something, a movement, the way the man's coat overlapped my leg, caused me to glance. He was middle-aged, as old as Father, perhaps, with small regular Irish features and a sunken drawstring mouth in the corner of which he held a burnt-out cigarette. Like Duffy, he was wearing a woolen cap. Once again engaged in the rough path that true love was taking on the screen, I did not at first feel the feathery exploration of my thigh, a tickle that came and went and that might have been my imagination. But then the tickling returned and stayed. I felt his fingers working.

"What. . . ?" I said aloud and drew away my leg.

"Sssh . . . sssh . . ." he said and lifted a finger of his other hand to his lips and with that "sssh" I was lashed to the seat. I could not have fled. It was too late, for already my blood (was it?) had galloped away. Moments later, the man stood abruptly and left the theater. On the screen, Allan Jones in his military uniform was pleading for sympathy. For a long time Jeanette would not relent, but then there was the power of the wound and soon their voices were soaring in the rapture of first love. "I/you want sympathy, sympathy . . ."

"Sssh, sssh," whispered Jeanette, her finger at Allan's lips, her eyes bottomless pools of sympathy.

It hadn't happened, I thought. It hadn't. The matinee over, the house lights went on. The audience departed. And still I sat in that theater that was like a premonition of death. All at once I heard a stern voice like that of the archangel pointing from the gates of Eden.

"You can't stay here. Time to go." It was the usher. I rose, bent as though I had been struck in the middle and slunk up the aisle. It was dark when I reached home. I was certain that the evidence was stamped on my face, that Mother would know at once what had happened. She had a sixth sense about wrongdoing. Guilt, she said, had a sharp sour smell, like geraniums. In the bathroom I checked the mirror to see if a mark had appeared on my forehead. There was none. Perhaps I was not doomed? Fifty years later another mirror shows a deep line rising from the bridge of the nose to slice my brow as with the blade of an ax.

"Your line of pain," said Janet, my wife.

"That's Cain," I corrected her.

For weeks I lived in terror of being found

out. There would be a knock at the door. The police would come. I would be led away in manacles, made to sit on the stool of penitence before all of Troy, like one of the common fornicators Mother accused Father of raising.

It is fifty years later and I refuse to elevate that poor man in Proctor's Theatre to the level of the satanic. I wish it had not happened. I did not need the anguish. Of that, my plate was already full. But with years have come understanding and the suspicion that we are all hiding the same things and are only different in the carrying out of them. Can one hate a man for taking what he desperately needed? No, for since then I have had a few crepuscular urges of my own. In the words of Emily Dickinson, "it was just a happen." I told no one, not even Billy. For all his "experience," he would have been floored. Besides, death had made us shy with each other. Certainly I could not have told Mother. I had long before stopped telling her the truth. She wasn't equipped to hear it. Would I have told Father? I think I would not. The men of Troy are not strong that way. But now here is a photograph of myself at age thirteen. I see a skinny, youngish old man wearing the dead smile of someone who has been through it all before. There is more boy in me now than there was then.

After Father's death, Grandpa refused to accept money from Mother for the cigarettes and whiskey that were his only pleasures. Unbeknownst to her, he took to roaming the streets, picking up cigarette butts and smoking them through his black-and-silver cigarette holder. In time, he became a familiar figure, dragging his immense inguinal hernia through downtown Troy, holding the bulge in with one hand while bending painfully to retrieve a prize with the other. For both of their sakes I hadn't the heart to tell Mother. It had become a compulsion, something he could not help doing. The one time I dared to remonstrate with him, he turned purple with rage; his head shook with it and swelled like a loaf of bread. I never said anything about it again. Eventually, of course, Mother was told. Mortified, she made him promise not to do it again. He simply must, she told him, accept the money. It was little enough. We could afford it, she lied. He did take the money, then furtively returned it each time to her purse. And he never stopped picking up cigarette butts from the street.

Grandpa continued to occupy his room on the first floor in back of the office. There the old king spent his days reading the Yiddish newspaper through a magnifying glass, wandering from his bed to the backyard, settling in among the shrubbery, inviting it to grow over him and speaking only a few words each day. He was to live so for another fifteen years. Mother wrote to me of his death when I was in Korea serving in the army. How one day, when he had not appeared for supper, she went to see, and found the room in a state of upheaval, the table overturned, and the lamp. Blood pooled on the floor; and fallen across the bed, my grandpa. A seizure, she wrote. The struggle, it must have been awful.

Within a year of Father's death, Mother

sprang up like a sapling that had been weighted down with snow. It was not that she had felt imprisoned by her household or by her role as the doctor's wife. It was simply that she was unsuited for the role of the widow, cherishing her sorrows like Aunt Sarah. If Fate had decreed that she be unmoored, why she would accept that and behave otherwise from then on. "Otherwise" involved a sea change in her personality. Always witty and stylish, she became flirtatious and coy. It had the inevitable result of making her popular with husbands, less so with wives.

Her smile became even more operatic, lit up by eyes of great lucency, a charming flash of white teeth. Her hair became something that Titian might have painted. A fox stole rested its head on one breast, its hind paws on the other. Had she been of the mineral kingdom, she would have been something made of cameo, ivory, tortoiseshell and mother-of-pearl. She grew slimmer.

"You are shrinking," I told her.

That laugh! "I have lost some avoirdupois. Never mind, I have a long way to go before I melt down to the original rib."

At sixteen Billy fled into the navy. That left Grandpa and me. It wasn't long before there were gentlemen callers: John, Max the First, Henry, Max the Second and the rest. What was it that brought the old dogs in such numbers to the doorstep? I shall try to be objective. Short of stature—just under five feet tall, rather too generously covered and with an ample bosom and long full dark hair, Mother had not beauty so much as the implication of it. More than that, she

gave off an aura that reassured a man she would
do whatever was necessary to shore up his masculinity. She had the kind of reciprocal mouth
that promised to give in return whatever was
given to it, and an improvisational speech spun
forth without forethought or censorship. Watching her present her cheek—one did not know
whether for a kiss or to take the air, one saw precisely why the sober men of Troy grew
lightheaded and glandular in her presence. She
was Woman—excessive, warm, vain, generous.
And not to be resisted.

Just beneath love lay worry. When she did
not come home at night, I paced the floor. Had
she met with an accident, been abducted, or
worse? When the time came to apply to college
and then to medical school, proximity was the
principle by which I was governed. How could I
leave her? Like Andromache after the slaying of
Hector, by whose step would she be gladdened?
For the next four years, I attended Union College, twelve miles away in Schenectady. After
that, there was Albany Medical College, closer by
six miles. Both schools proved happy choices,
combining excellence and generosity. Most important, if I hollered loud enough from either
one, she could hear me and rejoice. When I began my training in surgery in New Haven, Troy
seemed as far away as Angkor Wat.

Of the several suitors whom she went so far
as to marry, first was Henry. There came the day
six months later that Henry threatened her with
a kitchen knife. Within an hour, she put on her
hat, took my arm and we walked to the courthouse, where the surrogate informed her that

Henry was a well-known predator upon women. He had been arrested before for blackmail and extortion. The marriage was annulled, the man banished from Troy under threat of arrest if he returned.

John was a charming scamp with the map of Ireland on his face and a wife somewhere. An ex-vaudevillian, he did a soft-shoe around the dining-room table, wearing a bowler hat and spats and carrying a cane. Tongues wagged at Mother's "shenanigans." The doctor's wife! Through it all, our fortunes rose and fell, mostly fell. Between times, she sold stockings at Frear's department store. After school, I sold magazines, bagged groceries and worried. At home, I partook of her self-generated *joie de vivre* and did not report to her the gossip I overheard. She alternated between drawing me close and fending me off.

"Don't you ever become the confidant of women," she said. "I'm afraid you've got that in you. To play the eunuch or the clown in the hope you'll be flung a few bits of cast-off affection is silly." The real tragedy of Cyrano de Bergerac, she said, was not his unrequited love. It was that he valued himself so little as to be a go-between.

Billy, home on liberty from the navy, took a good look.

"Poor kid," he said to me. "It can't be easy living with King George the Fifth and Gloriana, the Faerie Queene." With his forget-me-not eyes and aureole of golden hair, Billy made his way around Troy like a Botticelli angel. Even the dogs followed him down the street. In the sanctuary of our bedroom, I asked him about "life."

"My idea of a perfect playmate," he pronounced, "is someone who is mentally above average and morally below it." With a quick pounce he was on top of me, pinning my arms and legs. "You need a girlfriend." He searched my face.

"Think so?"

"You're spending too much time by yourself."

"What's wrong with that?"

"One is known by the company he keeps."

"Get off me, you bum." I was trying not to cry. Then he was gone.

Had it all, everything that went before Father's death, been an impersonation? Still, Mother was capable of self-analysis.

"I'm not given to displaying my sons, only myself. I wouldn't subject you to the kind of gossip I seem to invite."

Max the First was a dour man with a chronically sulky expression relieved only by the sight of Mother. Max possessed an ileostomy, about which he had neglected to speak before they were married.

"What is that?" I wanted to know.

"It is an opening here . . ."

"But surely . . ."

"No. I cannot forgive the deception." The man pleaded against the divorce until it was decreed.

Three years later, after I had moved out, late one evening, the doorbell rang. It was Max the First. He was, Mother told me, clearly ill. Gasping, his skin gray and covered with sweat, one hand pressed to his chest, he fixed her with a terrible glittering eye like that of the Ancient Mariner and said nothing. Once in the parlor upstairs, he sank onto the couch and held out his arms to her. She went to him. Minutes later, he laid his head upon her breast and died. In the dormitory at college, the phone rang.

"Come home now," she said. I ran all the way to the bus station and caught the last bus from Schenectady to Troy. An hour later, I opened the unlocked door and raced up the stairs. She was still kneeling over him.

"I have been punished," she said, on her face a look of remorse.

"We'll see him buried," I told her and went to phone the undertaker. "I'll stay home till after that."

But enough. To mention the precise number of her amours would be "rude," in her mind. And so I shan't. What difference if it was three or twelve? The impertinence of mere numbers! Besides, by the time I graduated from medical school, it was all over, like a wrinkle that had been smoothed out. Either she had done with them or they with her. I didn't ask, only accepted with pleasure what had become mine again by default.

"My decade of folly," was all she said of it. Only once, many years later, did the subject come up.

"Did you love all those men?"

"They all loved me. For a while."

"I'm not at all surprised. And Father?" She held out her hand, thumb and forefinger separated by half an inch.

"I loved him just so much and not one jot
more. Let's not talk about that old stuff anymore." We never did again.

Now, patiently stalking the past, I do not
think of it harshly. Whatever anyone else made
of her, to me she was beyond reproach. Besides,
I knew something about her. The summer I
turned ten, two older women cousins came for a
visit. One night, when it was supposed we were
sound asleep in our room, that was only half
true. Billy was; I wasn't. Mother and Father had
gone out for the evening. Hearing the two cousins murmuring in the kitchen, and already addicted to eavesdropping, I crept from my bed to
listen outside the door. They were talking about
something terrible that had happened long ago
to a "young girl." It was some time before I realized that the young girl had been Mother. The
year was 1916. The place, Montreal. From a previous eavesdropping foray, I had learned that at
that time aliens by the thousands, many of them
stowaways from Eastern Europe, had sneaked
into Canada and disappeared into the teeming
ghetto of St. Urbain Street. Apparently it was not
so hard to do. But if you got caught, you were
deported. At about that time, Mother met a
young illegal immigrant named Louis. Handsome as coin, my cousins whispered, and with a
brilliant mind. The handsome part was later confirmed by a faded photograph I found among
Mother's effects. It showed a slender, brooding
black-haired young man. Before long, they had
fallen in love; marriage was spoken of. But Louis
was already coughing blood. His illegal status
made seeking medical attention risky. If it was

found out, he would be deported. As weeks passed and Louis's condition grew worse, Mother decided to take him to a clinic, where the diagnosis of tuberculosis was confirmed. It was the miliary kind, called then galloping consumption, that did not confine itself to the lungs but was spread by the bloodstream throughout the body. Louis was to be sent to one of the government sanatoriums that ringed Montreal, but in order for him to be admitted, a questionnaire had to be filled out. There was his essential foreignness, his ignorance of either English or French. Where was he staying? Who was supporting him? How and when had he come to Canada? In the end he was refused admission to the sanatorium. Furthermore, he was told he had to leave the country.

That very day, Mother packed a valise and the couple took a train, then a bus, until they reached Windsor, Ontario. They walked along the border until she saw a place to sneak across into Detroit, a city large enough to disappear into. There they lived in a furnished room in a poor neighborhood. All day, she nursed him. At night, she went out to sing in the saloons, then rushed home to nurse him again. It took Louis six months to die. When she made it back to Montreal, heartbroken at having to leave his corpse behind, Mother found herself in disgrace. A used woman! Who would marry her now?

The last winter I lived home, Mother came down with influenza. The illness was acute and severe. In her delirium she had cried out, "Louis!" When the fever had burned out, I sat by her bed reading to her or watching her face as she slept. When she was well, I asked her.

"Who is Louis?"

"Louis? I don't know any Louis."

"You called out 'Louis' in your dreams."

"That is a lie!" She was furious. "Why must you lie all the time? I can't imagine where you get it."

Four years after Louis's death, she was still singing, on the Montreal waterfront. Father was then a senior medical student at the McGill School of Medicine. One night he went to that bar with his friends and there she was, singing the "Kashmiri Love Song."

It took him, he said later, about ten minutes to tumble. That long? she would say, with a look of reproach. Who would marry her? Father would, that's who.

I don't know why, but I never told Billy or anyone else about Louis. Perhaps it was Harpocrates, the shushing god, who held his finger to my lips and sealed them until now. Nor do I know if Father knew. Somehow I think he did not. The women in our family kept a good many secrets. The same independence of spirit, call it defiance, that had caused her to elope with the dying Louis led her to reject the conventional notion of widowhood. Or was it the hypocrisy of mourning? There had been that other eavesdropped question, remember: "Then why did you marry me?"

Everything makes me think of her: the seventy-year-old Peruvian Indian who had walked twenty miles to the hospital in Arequipa, where I had gone to do surgery. She had come down from the mountains to have her cleft lip repaired.

"But why now?" I wanted to know. "You have lived with it so long."

"Because," she replied, "I do not want to go to Heaven like this."

It seemed a good enough reason to me. When I had operated and, later, when the stitches had been removed, I handed her a mirror. In that self-admiring glance, I caught the scent of Mother, her insistence that passion does not diminish with age, but grows stronger even on to the last passion of dying.

I found her reflection again at the Golden Grove convalescent home, where, since my retirement from medicine, I go once a week to trim toenails, change dressings, debride bedsores, talk, mostly listen. In a four-bed room, I was filing down the overgrown fungal toenails of an old woman who was oblivious of my presence. In the next bed, behind a drawn curtain, a nurse's aide was bathing an elderly woman. The aide, it seemed from her slow languid voice, was just passing the time, asking idle questions. But the old woman was fully alive, ready to tell. It was the aide who spoke first.

"What did you used to do, Lucille?"

"You mean before I had come to this place? You might say I was in relief."

"That's better than being *on* it. What did you relieve people of?"

"Dirt. Just like you, only I was a bath lady. It was my profession. Went around to people's houses and gave baths to the ones who couldn't bathe themselves."

"Gave baths? How'd you get into that?"

"Took care of my husband for two years before he died. One day I told him, 'Jimmy, you're ripe. I'm goin' to give you a bath.' And before he could raise Cain, I had a basin of hot water and we were in the suds. Did him up every day from then on till the day he died. 'Lucille,' he'd say to me, 'you've got sympathetic hands.' And when he'd go 'Aaah,' I'd know for sure that I was easing his path. Well, after Jimmy passed on, I needed a job but I didn't know how to do anything. Then I remembered what Jimmy said about my hands, that they were sympathetic. It was what he left me, you could say, instead of money, my inheritance. So I said to myself, Lucille, it is only natural for a woman to make use of her best points. So off I went to the Visiting Nurse Agency and said I wanted a job giving bed baths. Let's see, they said, and I showed them. And what do you know? They took me on. The first day they sent along a regular nurse to give me instructions. I had to laugh because by then there was nothing I didn't know about giving a bath. Some days, I gave as many as six, house to house, carrying my little black bag just like the doctor. Pretty soon they all knew me, could see me coming. 'Bath Lady's here!' The kids would shout into the doorway."

"Didn't it ever get boring? I mean just giving one bath after another?"

"Boring! I should say it did *not* get boring. Every single body is different, like a house you go into for the first time and have to find your way around, get to know where everything is. There's a lot to it—people don't realize. What with the rubdown and toenails and snipping hair out of noses, it took me an hour each one, top to bottom. I was particular. Never used anything but Ivory soap and Johnson's baby oil. And nothing with perfume in it for some poor soul to have to smell all day and night like it or not. A lot of them can't speak up and tell you. Boring! Just the opposite. You never knew what was going to happen. Like the time I walked in, said good morning, pulled down the sheet, picked up an arm, started washing and come to find out that arm was stone cold and the woman dead for hours. That's not what I call boring. Listen, you take a few old parcels of bedsores and bones lying all day in crumbs or worse and by the time you're done, kings and queens is what you've got. It was polish, polish, polish until they glowed. With each rub you could feel the blood coming closer to the surface. Calling it forth, I used to say. After a while I could tell who could take a good scrubbing and who got just a lick and a promise. A body'll tell you what it needs."

"Some are cranky, though. There's no pleasing some."

"That's where the fun comes in."

"Fun?"

"I had one old geezer. His wife would roll up her eyes. 'He's in a mood,' she'd say. 'Never mind,' I'd tell her. 'I'll do him up, he'll purr for you all day.' And then there's modesty. Some haven't been touched in years. Cover up what you don't need to get at is the way. Naked isn't nude. Anyone doesn't understand that doesn't belong in that profession."

"Anyone ever get fresh?"

"Oh that."

"Come on, Lulu, tell."

"There was one old man just had an operation for hernia and then got clots or something, a stroke. I can't remember. Anyway, he got ideas. Said a good thing he got his hernia fixed if he was going to carry me over the threshold. 'I'm not that fat!' I told him."

There was a prolonged silence. Then:

"You've turned awful quiet on me, Lucille. Just when it was getting good. What's on your mind?"

"I was just thinking."

"Come on! Tell. I won't tell a soul."

"Promise? Well, there was this one young man, Charlie. Only twenty-five or so, both arms in casts. Bone cancer, they said. I was giving him, you know, private care when I noticed hard evidence. I looked up and that boy was staring at me. Just staring. It wasn't shame, it was pleading."

"What did you do?"

"First thing I did, I went and closed the door. 'Never you mind,' I told him. 'Just another sore muscle to be done up.' That was the one and only time I extended, you might say, the limits of a bed bath. He died a few weeks later. And I've never been sorry I did it."

"Well, you're all clean, Lucille. How does it feel?"

"How do I feel? If I had wings, I'd spread 'em out and fly around the room three times."

What do you mean *if*, I thought from behind the curtain.

From the time I left for college in Schenectady, I received a weekly letter written in lavender ink in Mother's flourishing hand. They all contained at least one sentence that began with the phrase *Needless to say*. Occasionally, this was changed to *Suffice it to say* when the admonishment deserved a more severe tone of voice. "Suffice it to say, my darling, that you must not think of becoming a doctor. To follow in one's father's footsteps is thought by some to be an act of tribute. But in your case that would be a sentimental miscalculation. You are not suited for it. Besides, just look at what it did to your father." Thus did she continue the tug-of-war long after her opponent had let fall the rope from his lifeless fingers. The day I informed her that I had been accepted at Albany Medical College, she bowed to the inevitable but not before murmuring wistfully, yet again, "I had so wanted you to be a girl. But such was not given to me."

The weekly letters continued, although now the warnings dealt with such other pitfalls as premature emotional entanglements. "Rise and flee the reeling faun," she urged in one letter.

Then again, she was wildly inconsistent.

"You do not take enough chances," she wrote. "With you, it is all duty." And another time:

"You must learn to be absurd. Fling yourself away now and then. Surely I have shown you that."

Years later, after reading one of my memoirs of Troy, she wrote: "Needless to say, I am less than pleased. Why, in the name of God, do you always have to lie so? I can't imagine where you got it." Suffice it to say, I turned to give a courteous salute to the ghost of Duffy, the Bard of Troy. Was it a measure of our devotion that while I discarded all of her letters to me, she saved all of mine to her? Several months after her death I read them through, taking melancholy pleasure in the ones I had worked up into small conceits in order to make her smile. Here is one of her favorites:

Dearest Mother,

Of all the forms of literature, I love best to read collections of letters—those of Jane Carlyle to her husband, Thomas, those of Madame de Sévigné to her daughter, those of Charles Lamb to Coleridge, and the letters of Virginia Woolf to just about everyone. Reading letters is tantamount to eavesdropping. You can catch an otherwise sobersided man in a moment of frivolity, or a woman in hot pursuit of her heart's delight. It's always a terrible letdown when one of the correspondents goes to visit the other. Suddenly there are no letters to read. It is like having a door slammed in your face. What is a poor snoop to do but sit outside and imagine all the wickedness going on behind your back? Best of all, I love to read those letters found in the bottom drawer of an old dresser in the attic. Tied up in silk ribbon and written in pale lavender ink, there they have lain all those years, still redolent of passion, and all the while threatening to undergo spontaneous combustion and burn the house down.

I like to write letters too. But one of the few blessings denied me is an ideal correspondent. That "Dearest Friend" the presence of whose letter in my mailbox would bring forth a purr of anticipation as though it were a dish of cream to be lapped up. In the absence of such a person, I have hired on as my own "Dearest Friend." Oh I don't actually put them in an envelope, stamp and mail them, except for once or twice, but I have not had to stoop that low in years. Here in its entirety is one of those letters:

Dearest Friend,

I have been keeping company with Dr. Jacobs, my dentist, and so have been unable to answer your peevish letter. Dr. Jacobs is such a man as is given to little snorts and grunts at the same time as he roots about in my canals, as though there were a truffle at the bottom of each of my teeth. It is all done to the insectual whine of the air-turbine drill and the hiss and bubble of the saliva-ejector. To an ancient Babylonian resurrected from his tomb and brought to that office, it would doubtless appear that he had happened upon a strange exotic search for something that we had lost, with Dr. Jacobs looking for it in my mouth, and me looking up his nose. During my Passion Dr. Jacobs entertains me with the dental catechism, much of which has to do with the avoidance of everything I like to smoke, eat and drink and the absolute moral responsibility of every man, woman and child to floss. I would gladly lay down my life if it would preserve the English language from contamination by that awful verb *to floss*. There are certain disgusting physical acts which no one ought to be called upon to do. Flossing is one of them. I am of the simple persuasion that tooth decay is not a moral issue. Pain, after all, is a teacher. Do we not all decay?

Today I told Dr. Jacobs about St. Apollonia, the patron saint of dentists and of those who suffer from toothache. She it was, I told him, who in the course of her third-century martyrdom, had each one of her teeth pulled out ... without novocaine. To this bit of dentiana, Dr. Jacobs responded by snorting even more loudly into my jaws. Then he resumed his dreary litany, offering now a sorrowful "oy," now a sigh of Old Testament proportions. As though my dental cavities were related to the decay of Western civilization!

I am beginning to suspect that Dr. Jacobs is a tooth fetishist. I very much fear that one day it will all come out in the open. He will have gone too far, walked around town rattling a pocketful of teeth, now and then taking them out to play with. That sort of thing. Again and again, I have admonished him not to let any of *my* teeth fall into enemy hands. It is well known that teeth are a symbol of a man's strength and sexual prowess. All this I told him. Once again he failed to respond. Is the man deaf?

"You should get a parrot for your waiting room," I said. "Like Dr. Brecht, the dentist in *Buddenbrooks*."

"They are filthy, unsanitary birds," he said.

"You could teach it to say: 'Floss three times a day.'"

"Open," he said. I could hear his quick anticipatory breaths. In the sudden brightness of my mouth, he squinted and shaded his eyes with one hand like an explorer who breaks from a forest upon a vast golden savannah.

"Yours is one of the worst mouths I have ever seen," he said.

"My life," I replied, "has not been without oral adventure."

The real horror of the dentist's chair is neither his pliers nor his drill. I could bear both, I think, with dignity. It is Dr. Jacobs himself that makes me call out for general anesthesia.

Faithfully yours,

P.S. If you think me a meanspirited correspondent, just think of King David, who lusted after Bathsheba, the wife of Uriah. Here is the letter that David wrote, sealed and gave to Uriah himself to hand-carry to Joab, the Israelite general who was off fighting the Philistines:

"Set ye Uriah in the forefront of the hottest battle and retire ye from him that he may be smitten and die."

Frankly, I wouldn't trust a psalmist as far as I could throw him.

Your loving son,

And this:

Dearest Mother,

Of course you remember *vaccimulgence*. It was the only time I bested Billy in a word-fight. I reminded him of it yesterday on the telephone. Can you believe that sore loser is still smarting over it? What! You don't remember? Then I must remind you too. The word comes from the Latin *vacca* meaning cow (as in vaccination) and from *mulgere* which is the verb *to milk* (as in emulsify) ergo *vaccimulgence*—the milking of cows. I suppose it wasn't really fair of me to use it, but then . . .

I had found the word in a letter written by the very young Samuel Taylor Coleridge to his best friend in which he asked him to be on the lookout for a fit servant, "someone expert in vaccimulgence." Come to find out, it wasn't in the dictionary. Coleridge had made it up. For fifty years I have cherished the secret ambition to be the *second* person ever to use *vaccimulgence* in a sentence. Artfully, that is. None of your "I came upon a pretty girl drowsy at her vaccimulgence." No, that simply won't do. After dozens of false passages, I am pleased to report that I at last have realized my ambition. Here is a little story entitled Vaccimulgence. You must tell me what you think.

Vaccimulgence

Even before she opened the barn door, Audrey knew from the sound of rhythmic pissing into a zinc pail exactly what she would see. Her husband, Roger, sitting on a three-legged stool, his forehead pressed into the flank of a cow, absorbed in the tactile mysteries of vaccimulgence. It occurred to her that it had been years since he had touched her with anything near that tenderness.

Either he had not heard her footsteps behind him or he had and chose to ignore. Whatever. Roger remained as he was and gave no sign. From where she stood, Audrey could see his elbows working, working. The metallic whine of the milk hitting the side of the pail was the most hateful sound of her life.

At that moment, she could not have drifted from her purpose even had reason returned. No! She had come to the barn to kill and kill she would. She was no more than twenty feet from where Roger sat when she raised the barrel of the shotgun and fired. At the blast, the body of the man was flung from the stool, then lifted into a crouching position. The sudden movement overturned the pail. In a moment the floor of the barn at his feet was running with blood and milk. And slowly, as in a dream, he turned to gaze down at the lifeless body of his beloved cow.

"Elsie!" he sobbed. "Why? Why?"

"She had it coming," said Audrey, "but I could never expect *you* to understand that."

THE END

Mother wrote back that she was delighted with the brevity of the story, which partially balanced out the vanity of its author. To which I wrote the following response:

Dearest Mother,

To hell with criticism; praise is good enough for me.

Your loving son,

Chapter 10

March 23, 1986

A call from George, the last of my stepfathers. Mother has had a stroke. Three and a half hours later, I arrive at the Samaritan Hospital in Troy to find her sitting up in bed looking tiny and vague and with her hair hanging long and free like a young girl gone prematurely gray, her personality lying about her like crumbs in the bed.

George and Uncle Frank are in the room, two old men, both of them well into their eighties. They begin to cry as soon as they see me. Not so much, I think, out of worry or relief as from the sense that my having come lends the matter solemnity. If I have come, things must be pretty bad. Mother can't speak but from her expression, the same look she had on the stage of the Troy Music Hall in the role of Lily in *The Golden Links of Love Are Broken,* I can tell the soubrette knows me. It is pitiful to see her all deflated (without a bit of her flair), half of her chest flat where cancer had got at it, and her not able to see about her prosthesis. She shakes her head and rummages about in her mind for a word but can't find so much as *and* or *but* until all of a sudden out comes, "Jesus Christ Almighty!" Plain as day. Frank, George and I laugh out loud to see that blasphemy is what comes back first. Mother looks from one to the other and gives the sweetest smile in North America and then we all have a good cry.

"If that woman ain't a witch, what is she?" says George.

"A good thing you weren't born three hundred years ago," I tell her. "You'd have been burned at the stake." In the solarium, George informs me he heard the teacup fall and knew at once.

"She don't drop teacups," he says. It was just like Mother to announce her stroke with the tinkle of a teacup slipping from her lap to the floor. By rights it should have been a bugled fanfare that called such a lyrical brain into lethargy.

March 30, 1986

Mother is regaining her speech, according to George. The aphasia is clearing. Would it hurt the world, I ask you, if she were permitted to live another few years with her faculties intact?

October 7, 1986

About Mother, she is what some call dead. I suppose I should have known. There were omens, had I been receptive: a line of migrating geese that wavered and broke like a sudden arrhythmia on an electrocardiogram. And the day before, I had run over a cat.

How old was she? In our family, it has always been considered bad manners to know the exact age of one's mother. But *entre nous* she was just a girl of eighty-eight. Sometimes, secure in the knowledge that I would lie in her favor, she would put the question.

"How old do you think I am?"

"Oh, I don't know. Somewhere in the sixties."

"Right on the button," she would marvel, then lift that famous forefinger to scold.

"But it is wicked of you to know. Tell it not in Gath."

"Why not?"

"Lest the daughters of the uncircumcised find out and rejoice."

I ought to have known in June, when she phoned on my birthday. I picked up the receiver and there she was giving me the first three measures of "O mio babbino caro" in that soprano that sounded as though a white mouse were ringing a little silver bell. I waited till she was through.

"You remembered," I said.

"How old are you anyway?" she asked. She knew darn well.

"I'm fifty-eight," I told her.

"If that is so," she said importantly, "then I am an old woman." That was the first time she had ever allowed it.

"Are you feeling all right?" I asked.

And then there was last Sunday. I called her up.

"Autumn," she said. "I wasn't expecting it so soon." And with studied nonchalance, "I've decided to turn over an old leaf."

"What's that supposed to mean?" But I already knew.

"You'll see," she said.

"Don't! I am not ready!"

"Oh, you! You'll never be ready. You have got to be more philosophical. Death is the prize to which we can all aspire." I could just see her scratching in her hair with a pencil and looking out the window at the foliage. An hour later I was in the car and headed upstate. Never, never had there been so much red on the trees. Each gust sent more of it spattering. At the rest stop, I walked into the woods a bit, knelt to dip my fingers in the fallen leaves. By the time I got to Troy, she was in the intensive-care unit, having achieved a myocardial infarction big enough to turn her nose blue. But sizing me up, I could tell.

"You're holding your belly button," she said. It took her six breaths to get it out.

"I've got a pain in it," I told her. She responded by rolling up her eyes the way she did, commercing with the skies.

"You'll get over it," she gasped.

In the corridor, Billy, the doctor and I discussed the case. Soberly, sensibly, like professionals.

"No," Billy answered him. "No resuscitation, no tubes, no respirator. Let her be."

"That is wise," said the doctor. "She has been wanting to die for fifteen years that I know of."

Billy and I stood on either side of the bed all night. Toward dawn, she opened her eyes.

"Ivy," she said. It was her last word.

"I.V.," said Billy. "The intravenous is bothering her." He went to get the nurse. But I knew better. Ivy in a cemetery takes care of itself; there's no need to plant flowers every little while and you need not worry about it being the wrong color.

"Yes," I said. "Ivy would be best." But she was already out of earshot. When it came, that last breath, it was as though a lamp in whose circle of light I had lived all my life had been extinguished. Now I was free to live anywhere. In the dark.

The day of the funeral it rained. I wasn't surprised. The town knew what it had lost. All about us the cemetery was doing what it does, gravely regarding. No stone but bowed its head in welcome. From the road, we watched the men carry her toward Father. It was not smooth sailing, what with the path all muddy and rutted. The coffin swam jerkily like some blind homing creature that would have to find its way by instinct. Never mind—she knew where to go. There was the trench, like a socket from which the tooth had been pulled. Then the ancient spectacle, full of murmuring and slow gestures. The village of black umbrellas.

As there are smells that have the power to awaken the distant past, so are there sounds. When Billy and I sank the shovel into the mound of earth and threw it on the coffin, the noise of the clods striking wood, the way they scattered a bit at the end of each thud, I remembered how forty-five years ago in this very spot Billy and I—he fourteen, I twelve—shoveled earth on Father, each time stiffening against the wince, feeling the thrust of the shovel in our sides as though our own flesh were being turned into that trench. It is the most serious, the most prophetic sound of one's life. Now here was Mother, so eager for death she would have pulled the earth over herself if we had faltered. Even before we had finished, leaves fell into the grave until it was bright as ruby, as topaz. In the late afternoon, Billy and I drove to Fifth Avenue between Jacob and Federal to see our old house.

"That place could use a coat of paint," I said.

"What a dump," said Billy.

"It's your native land," I remonstrated.

"It's a dump," he repeated.

"A man turns his back on his native land at his own risk." We walked around back to see the old empty lot.

"Our baseball field," I said. "They've paved it."

"What do you mean 'our'? *You* never came out to play. Always stayed inside reading the *Odyssey* or the *Iliad* or something equally irrelevant."

"It was the only homer I could ever hit." The way he said *"you"* I could tell he was crying. We walked down to the river, which was steaming like the pale belly of a horse. Or were those fumes from a just-fed altar?

"That dumb doctor said she wanted to die," I began.

"That she did," said Billy. "She was dog tired of hanging on for your sake."

"I don't believe you," I said.

Billy eyed me critically. "You know, for all your reading Homer, you don't know much." We walked back to the car.

"What's your version of the hereafter?" I asked him.

"I believe," he said, "that some portion of the person persists in some undefined way."

"That's dumb," I told him. "Mine is that it is best not to be cremated so that when the Messiah comes you can be ready to get up and follow Him intact to the Promised Land."

"Will you stop!" said Billy, and that was that.

At the house we studied the death certificate and the bill for the funeral. The death certificate bore four signatures: Mark W. Levine, the funeral director; Catherine A. O'Bryan, who issued the "removal permit"; Cydne R. Brown, the registrar of vital statistics; and a doctor whose name was not legible. The bill for the funeral included money for two women to wash and enshroud, and one woman to sit up all night with the body. Billy said it looked okay to him.

That night I fell asleep thinking about the Sunday afternoon last June when Mother and I had gone for a stroll downtown. She was wearing white gloves and carrying her parasol. Believe you me, she could have given master classes in how to open and twirl that thing. At the corner of Congress and River streets she paused.

"Do you think Troy has changed much since your last visit?"

I had been there only six weeks earlier. "Eternal Troy," I said. "Jerusalem of my soul." And waited for what I knew was coming.

"There are many Athens," she said, "but only one Troy." It was her favorite joke. We sauntered on to the Hendrik Hudson Tea Room, where for the umpteenth time she introduced me to Gloria, the waitress.

"This is my son," she announced. "With a *u*."

Gloria beamed on cue. "What'll you have today, Gertrude? The usual?"

"Hot, hot tea and two ladyfingers." As though *hot, hot* were twice as hot as *hot*. "The water must be boiling when it strikes the tea leaves."

"And sunny boy?"

"Bourbon," I said. "Cold, cold. And skip the ladyfingers." When Mother laughed, there was that white mouse still ringing a silver bell.

My having been born of her did not shut the gate between us as friends. We each knew to expect lies from the other—benevolent, colorful lies about the past. No grown-up proper view of what had once been, but a romantic fiction. Now we looked forward to hearing it for the hundredth time.

And underneath the banter and nostalgia lay the confidence that no matter what the folly or miscalculation, we would find motives for each other—to excuse, to exculpate. Above all, we offered each other the opportunity to behave well. Such a thing is to be found only once, if ever, in any lifetime.

Before heading back to New Haven the day after the funeral, I thought, Well, why not? And drove up to the cemetery. There was the clatter of cold metal as I turned the big old key in the iron gate. The path was still muddy from yesterday's rain but there were islands for hopping. I stopped before the fresh mound of earth.

"Okay," I said aloud. I was all business. "I've got my notebook and my pencil and now I am ready." I opened the notebook on the flat top of Father's gravestone. It was a congenial height for writing. As though he approved.

"No more fooling around," I said to her.
"All that jauntiness, while all the time you were
unhappy and only I didn't know. Or wouldn't.
Well, thank you for that, but now it's my turn.
I'm going to reinvent your life. For a writer no
life is beyond repair. How would you like it to
go? I can start from the beginning or pick it up
anywhere along the line. Want to sing *Aida* at the
Met? Be declared the goddess of Quelque-chose?
No problem. All you have to do is tell me what
you would have wanted, what sorrows avoided,
what joys fulfilled. Don't worry about style.
That's my department, as music, you always said,
was yours, thank you. And not to worry, it isn't
going to be any mausoleum of words. If you co-
operate, I'll reconsider the working title: *Memoirs
of a Girl of Eighty-eight*. I'll be back in a few weeks
with the rough draft."

The ride home through those beloved coun-
ties was surprisingly lighthearted. How gentle
the countryside near Troy, with much farming
everywhere. Farming gives a sense of health to
the land. It is replenishing to watch at dusk while
a herd of cattle flows toward the barn. First one
cow advances. She pauses. Another thrusts
ahead, pulling the others behind it, until the last
one, trailing milk, is inside the barn. Along the
banks of the Hudson River the locust trees have
grown very tall. Their bark is thrown into deep
folds coated with lichen and moss. So old are
these trees that, without the least wind, one will
drop off a quite large branch as if to shed part
of its burden. This letting-fall doesn't seem to do
the tree any harm. It is more an anatomical relin-
quishment of a part so that the whole might re-

main healthy, much as a diabetic will accept the amputation of a gangrenous toe in order that he might once again walk upon his foot. How clever of these locust trees to require no surgeon for their trimmage, only their own corporeal wisdom.

Chapter 11

This happened once: I was working in the surgical clinic of the hospital in New Haven. A man about my age lay on the examining table in a cubicle. He was naked save for a johnny shirt (and was covered with a sheet). I introduced myself.

"Selzer? How do you spell that?" He wanted to know. I told him.

"Used to be a doctor up in Troy," he said. "Same name as yours. He fixed my hernia when I was a kid. Oh, forty some years ago." He pulled down the sheet and lifted the hem of his garment to show me the barely perceptible white scar in his groin, a mark that was to me like a hieroglyph in a stone I had found in the middle of a plain in Asia Minor. All at once, the cubicle and everything in it seemed to waver and glow as if seen through tears. For a long moment I stood motionless, with the sense that this event was taking place in an hour that would not pass. Whatever else in life would happen and be gone, this man, his scar, would exist always.

"He was my father," I said after a while.

"A good doctor," he said. "A good man." I began to debride the venous stasis ulcer on his leg. "Think it's going to heal, Doc?"

I told him it would, that I had seen many worse ulcers heal right up. I applied the bandage. He got up and began dressing.

"You ever hear of Hermes?" I had to ask. He hadn't. "He was the messenger of the gods, wore sandals with wings so he could fly. He was the one who taught Hippocrates the secrets of doctoring. I don't know why but you remind me of him."

"I'll take a pair of those wings," said the man.

For the next twenty years I was to devote myself to the craft of surgery, stuffing my fingers with mechanical ingenuity, until I was that piece of machinery called surgeon. My reading was confined to medical textbooks and journals. There seemed no time to read anything that did not immediately pertain to the care of patients. Nor did I feel the least hunger for the literature with which my boyhood had been nourished. It is the story of most doctors, and is responsible for the narrowness of vision and the robotic lack of imagination of those in the medical profession.

For the first two years of medical school I dissected the cadaver, learned the biochemistry and physiology of the organs and peered into Father's old monocular microscope, now and then letting my lips rest against the instrument, where I imagined his mouth had brushed it years before. Of those two years what I remember most clearly is the drudgery, the learning by rote of all those formulae, the stultifying effect of cramming.

My first contact with living patients came in the electroshock psychiatric clinic. It was the duty of the second-year medical students to attend the outpatient electroshock clinic. In a large room in the basement of the Albany hospital, fifty cots had been set up in rows. The room had the unvarnished monotony of an army barracks. At one end of the room on a sort of dais stood a high cable covered with a sheet. It was to this table that the patients were led in turn, first to step on the footstool, then to lie down. Once there, each was given first a bolus of intravenous sodium pentothal, and a moment later a wallop of electric current delivered through padded electrodes to the temples. To the uninitiated this clinic could have been taking place in a dungeon where political prisoners were being interrogated. It was our job to assist the patients onto the table, inject the pentothal and then steady them through the convulsion lest they be fractured or otherwise injured. Muscle relaxants were not à la mode. It was said by those in charge that the patients were amnesic for the seizure, remembered nothing. But we weren't so sure. Why, then, did so many balk and jib like cattle at an abattoir? Why did they dread it so? "Come, come," we would coax them. "Don't you want to feel better? It doesn't hurt." Perhaps it was the aching of their muscles afterward that told them of the violent way they had been used. Perhaps it was an intuition that their dignity had been taken away from them. But certainly they did not go gently.

At the flick of the switch, the patients would arch so that only occiput and heels were in contact with the table; arms and legs were thrust into a rigid shaking. Teeth clenched about a wooden tongue depressor padded with tape; all the muscles of the face and neck were engaged; the mouth worked, the eyelids did hard fluttering; the breath was suspended for endless seconds. Urine and semen were squeezed from the body and dark stains spread on the front of the johnny shirts they wore. Not so abrupt as the onset was the descent from convulsion. With the return of respiration, the whole body slumped, softened. Saliva foamed from nostrils and mouth. Seconds after the storm had passed, small colonies of muscle about the eyes and mouth twitched on, before at last they, too, winked out. When all was still, we would move the patients to one of the nearby cots, where nurses guarded them until they roused to a kind of floppy drunkenness. After an hour or two they were helped to dress and allowed to leave in the custody of next of kin. Calm, obedient, erased. The following week they would return for another convulsion. To us, in our second year of medical school, it was a reenactment of Dante's *Inferno*. In another part of the hospital, we were told, prefrontal lobotomy was being performed, an operation in which a clever little pick is passed through a hole in the skull and an ingenious cut made to tame a wild brain.

After two years, there came the thrill of

studying physical diagnosis, in which we learned how to examine the living body. Fitted out with the stethoscope, percussion hammer, wisps of cotton and a small plastic ruler, and with my pocket handbook of signs and symptoms, I conducted my first interrogations of the sick, learned just how to position a patient so as to better feel the edge of a spleen, palpate the pulses in the arch of the foot, search for the nodules of gout in the pinna of the ear and listen to what the patient was telling me, sensing somehow that only the sick had the power to know what was going wrong with them, begging forgiveness of the patients for whatever pain I caused them by my clumsiness, thanking them for putting up with the nuisance and pocketing each bit of new knowledge as though it were a nugget of gold with which I would one day ransom a human being back from the dead.

For twenty years I practiced and taught surgery, until at the age of forty my appetite for literature quite suddenly reappeared. And with it, the psychic energy to write down some of the dozens of short stories of which a doctor's daily round is made up.

The first of my stories was a retelling of the biblical tale of Jonah and the whale. Aside from the pleasure in describing the gastric mucosa of the beast that was Jonah's new home, there was the joy in telling a story. The choice of Jonah was perhaps not an accident, for it is the quintessential story of surgery. Jonah is the surgeon who enters the body of the patient/whale, dwells there until his destiny is fulfilled, then is cast forth while the whale swims off, healed. There fol-

lowed several years in which each night I wrote
horror stories in an attempt to gain some mas-
tery of sentence structure, syntax, narration. I
chose the horror genre first because it is the least
complex of fictions, requiring no great character
development, no philosophical profundities. The
goal of the horror story is visceral, to make the
reader shudder. I suppose that I was indulging
my own taste for the macabre and the grotesque.
Between the hours of one and three in the morning, when I was not on duty at the hospital, I sat
in the kitchen scribbling, with the rest of the
world asleep and all the light in the universe directed down upon a blank sheet of paper. In
time I learned the strength of words, how they
could raise you up high, higher than you deserved, how they could convince others to love
you, to do your bidding, how they could deflect
wrath. I became a manipulator of words—a
writer.

The year is now 1991. It is six years since I
retired from the practice and teaching of surgery. It was writing that made me do it. For sixteen years I had done both. Why not continue?
Would I have anything to write about if I with-
drew from surgery? Cut off from my source,
would I not be rendered impotent? Nor did I
walk away from the beloved workbench of my
life with a cheery wave of a hand. I knew only
that it was time to go. In the operating room the
patient is anesthetized so he will feel no pain.
The surgeon, too, must be in a sense anesthetized so he can be at some remove from the emotional heat of the event. After all, take away the

purpose of the surgery, and the laying open of the body of a fellow human being becomes an act of assault and battery. Throughout his long period of training, the surgeon dons a carapace that serves to insulate him from horror. The writer wears no such carapace but must perceive events and report them back to the waiting world in the most compelling language he can find. The surgeon who writes must not only perform the deed but perceive it fully, thus stripping off his own insulation, weakening his resolve. It was time to go.

For these six years, retired behind a quiet, unmolested door, recombining words and sentences into stories, I still have attacks of longing for surgery. What I miss most is the privilege of touching my fellow man in order to diagnose and to heal, but also I miss the teaching of surgery, which is like teaching nothing else. There, on either side of a narrow table, stand surgeon and pupil. Lying upon the table, plunged into magical sleep, lies the patient. It is the teacher's charge to act with all his skill in behalf of the unconscious person. It is no less his charge to pass on to the new doctor the secrets of this craft. The teacher must give rein to his student to the full extent of his abilities while at the same time checking him moments before harm will have been done. It is a state of the most delicate resonance. Above and within the body of the sleeping patient, four hands move, never losing contact with one another, while in low voices the age-old questions are asked and answered. Such is the murmuring, tactile pedagogy of surgery that satisfied my spirit for three decades.

Mother and Father, the beloved antagonists of Troy, are long since dead. Of all the satisfactions of my life, greatest is that I have at last fulfilled each of their ambitions.

Now, having practiced both surgery and writing, I am struck as much by the similarities between the two vocations as by their differences. A surgeon is apt to think of both in terms of instruments and physical activity. In the carrying out of each, a tool is held in the hand: In surgery this is a scalpel, in writing, a pen. In the use of one, blood is shed; in wielding the other, ink is spilled upon a page. In surgery the tissues of the body are sutured; in writing, words are stitched into sentences. The resemblance is further heightened in that the subject of my writing has so often been my work as a doctor. To render these events into story and essay I have made use of the diagnostic process. In attempting to solve an essay or a story, a writer will often entertain several possibilities before selecting the most appropriate one. This is not unlike the process of differential diagnosis, in which the doctor lists the most likely causes of a disease based on the oral history of the patient and the results of the tests and X rays. Often the list can be narrowed down to two or three possibilities. Pain in the lower right abdomen of a female patient is likely to be either appendicitis or a ruptured cyst of the ovary. Here is Juliet, commenting on the appearance of Romeo: "Either mine eyes deceive me, or thou lookst pale." And Groucho Marx, shambling into a room, trips over the body of a man lying on the floor. Groucho reaches for the pulse of the man and for a long moment studies his watch, counting. "Either this man is dead," he says at last, "or my watch has stopped."

A diagnosis, like a poem or a song, is a thing made. In medicine, diagnosis is often a matter of metaphor, making comparisons. It is an ancient human habit. When something—a rash, a cough, a fever—is *like* something else, it can be precisely identified. Faced with a difficult diagnosis, Father was given to muttering under his breath: "Looks like . . ." or "Reminds me of . . ." or "What do we have here?" I understood that these asides were rhetorical—part of the search for assurance. I was not supposed to answer. The one time I did—it just came blurting out—was in the emergency room of St. Mary's, where Father was attending the victim of a car accident. From the foot of the stretcher I watched him take hold of the covering sheet and lower it to expose the man's chest. A number of ribs on either side had been broken. The chest of the man did not rise and fall with his efforts to breathe, but some ribs rose while others fell at the same time. The sternum seemed to flail from side to side.

"Now what do we have here?" muttered Father to himself.

"Looks like a sprung umbrella, all its struts broken," I said aloud. On the way home that night, Father reached out and placed his hand on mine.

"He was awake, you know. I'm sure he heard you." I know now that a person cannot die of shame. Because I would have died then.

Sometimes it happens that while writing, I will make a simile or a metaphor in my mind and feel his hand on mine, staying it, hear his voice remonstrating, teaching me that writing, like doctoring, has nothing to do with cleverness. It is all diagnosis and feeling. It occurs to me that the storyteller may be less human than the doctor, who wrestles death to the mat each day; the storyteller is doomed to live as two, with one self laughing and weeping, and the other seated in a corner making theater of the event.

Both writing and surgery are concerned with wounds. The surgeon makes an incision, which is a purposeful wound in the body. Through this opening he will explore the interior, reading the entrails, as it were, in order to foretell the future of his patients. Long before there was paper and ink, a writer took up instruments and carved hieroglyphics in flat stone. These legible wounds comprised the earliest literature. While it is no longer necessary to gouge markings in order to tell a story, it requires no great leap of the imagination to see the words written on a page as purposeful wounds, equally capable of inflicting pain and of healing. With each word set down upon a page, the writer spends a bit of himself. He does this gladly, out of a desire to make something. Still, it is a self-destructive act, for, should that wound heal, the writer would be no more. Healing would have brought about the state of finality and fossilization in which writing could not be done.

One purpose of an essay is to unite the outside world, all of its objects and events, with the intimate dreams of the reader. A surgeon writing must be indulged if he sees the external in terms of human anatomy. My writing desk, for one:

This desk at which I've been sitting for sixteen years is about as far from a Louis XV secretaire as you can get. It is a rough, some might say charmless, piece of oak. All that remains of the great tree from which it descended is a kind of mute, patriarchal solidity. I found the desk at a public sale in which the furnishings of a house were being offered. It cost one hundred dollars. If wood were valued by the pound, this would have been a real bargain, for it required all the strength of four young men to carry it upstairs. In order to get it into my study, the door and its jamb had to be removed, then nailed back afterward. There never has been any question about its leaving that room. From that moment, my desk and my study were sealed in time and eternity. I do not know its age or whether anyone else has ever used the desk for writing. I think not, since the desktop has never been planed or sanded smooth. The surface is as ribbed and rutted as an old dirt road. Any letter written on it would give the impression of having been wrought by an elderly, tremulous hand. I like to think of myself as this desk's first occupant. That it and I had been waiting for each other for years. And if a piece of furniture can be said, the way it is said of a dog, to take on the features of its owner, why that is true of my desk, which is, like me, a pile of flat skeletal planes and right angles. There are no curves, no roundness, not the least bit of ornamentation. The brass drawer handles have so enjoyed the devotion of neglect that they no longer reflect the light, if ever they did.

Speaking of drawers, there are four on either side of the kneehole and a wide, shallow drawer that forms the roof of that space. Because it possesses no backboard, there are no sweet little cubbyholes for your odds and ends, your gewgaws. At any given time the desk is piled high and otherwise strewn with papers, books, photographs, pencils, pens—all the *rejectimenta* of the writer's craft. Only a page-sized space, front and center, is kept clear for the work of the moment. So high have these mountains of paper and books grown that, once seated, I cannot be seen by the intruder from whom I am known to hide and who has been known to barge right in and peer over the barricade to ascertain whether I am there or not. It has happened that a sudden avalanche will carry a section of the range tumbling to the floor, where it is likely to remain until I miss something and then must search among the rubble on hands and knees. As for the kneehole, it is capacious enough but sufficiently closed in to give a feeling of snugness. One's knees huddle there like sheep in a cote. So imagine a sleepy old desk, homely and patient, that suffers its burden of books, the endless shuffling of papers, the scratching of a pen. A perfect servant of a desk, you say.

But this desk has a secret. One of the right-hand bank of drawers, the second from the bottom, cannot be opened. Years ago, how many I cannot say, it became stuck shut with all the adhesive force of which matter is capable. Try as I might, I have never been able to pull it open. I am not, after all, Prince Arthur at the hilt of Excalibur. But once, I swear it, that drawer had

been open. I had placed things in it, taken things
out. But that was long ago. And now I can no
longer remember what lay within at the fateful
moment when the drawer shut itself up forever
and ever. In the years since, whenever I lose
something and after searching unsuccessfully for
hours, I come to the suspicion that it is there, in
that mule of a drawer. In order to accommodate
the lost articles I have over the years assigned to
that drawer, it would have to be the size of a
freight car. Therein lie, so near and yet so far,
the many essentials of my life, never to be
brought to light and forever endowed with all
the mystery of the invisible.

Once, in a rage of frustration, I cursed and
kicked the drawer, then ran to the basement for
an ax. But in the end it was not in me to demol-
ish a desk that had become for me my nest, my
lair, my cocoon, my egg, my cottage. In time, I
came to respect the privacy of that shut drawer
and, if anything, to love my desk all the more for
it. Such is the perverse nature of the human
heart. And more than once, while struggling to
find just the right words, I think I hear a murmur coming from that drawer as though something in it were giving me a hint.

What was once an unreachable, hated place
has become the locked drawer of my dreams,
in which all the beloved keepsakes of my life
dwell with one another. There, the lock of hair
of someone who loved me in a former life.
There, the scraps of paper upon which I have
written my secret desires, my most immortal
sentences, the manuscript of a tale of love and
death that would have melted the heart of

Bluebeard. To tell the truth, I wouldn't open that drawer if I could, not for all the world. In the sweet fatigue of old age, I have developed a sensuous love for the unseen. Also, I am not prepared to risk finding in that drawer none of my treasures but only a few paper clips, the stub of a pencil, twelve cents and a 1968 season ticket to the New Haven Symphony. If I have learned anything from my desk, it is that there are always more things in a stuck drawer than in one that you can open. It makes me think of surgery. For a surgeon, the abdomen is a closed drawer. The moment the abdomen is open, the outside world is effaced with a single stroke. An atmosphere of novelty and surprise reigns, for this drawer is full of jewels of unimagined splendor, inestimable worth. It is a writing surgeon's work to inventory this treasure and, more, to lead the reader into the interior so that he too can experience this mysterious place of his secret dreams. Listen:

One enters the body in surgery as in love, as though one were an exile returning at last to his hearth, daring uncharted darkness in order to reach home. Turn sideways, if you will, and slip with me into the cleft I have made. Do not fear the yellow meadows of fat, the red that sweats and trickles where you step. Here, give me your hand. Lower between the beefy cliffs. Now rest a bit upon the peritoneum. All at once, the gleaming membrane parts, and you are in. It is the stillest place that ever was. Why, when the blood sluices fierce as Niagara, when the brain teems with electricity and the numberless cells exchange their goods in ceaseless commerce, why is it so quiet? Had some priest in charge of these rites uttered the command "Silence"? This is no silence of the vacant stratosphere, but the awful quiet of ruins, of rainbows, full of expectation. Touch the great artery, feel it bound like a deer in the might of its lightness and know the thunderless boil of the blood. Lean for a moment against this bone. It is the only memento you will leave to the earth. Its tacitness is everlasting. Press your ear against this body the way a child holds a seashell and hears faintly the half-remembered, longed-for sea. Now strain to listen past the silence. In the canals, cilia paddle quiet as an Iroquois canoe. Somewhere nearby a white whip slide of tendon bows across a joint. Now there *is* sound, small splashings, tunneled currents of air. Slow, gaseous bubbles ascend through dark, unlit lakes. Across the diaphragm and into the chest: Here at least it is all noise, the whisper of the lung, the *lub-dup, lub-dup* of the garrulous heart. Such a primitive place. One expects to find drawings of buffalo on the walls. The sense of trespassing is heightened by the world's light illuminating the organs, their secret colors revealed, maroon and salmon and yellow. An arc of the liver shines high on the right like a dark sun. It laps over the pink sweep of the stomach, from whose lower border the gauzy omentum is draped and through which veil one sees sinuous, slow as just-fed snakes, the indolent coils of the intestine.

Once he has been led back out and the abdomen has been closed, the reader will go on dreaming of that place, the things he saw inside, and with even greater power because his imagination has been set in motion. There will always be more things in a closed abdomen than in an open one. To verify images kills them. It is always more enriching to imagine than to experience.

A surgeon knows little of art; it is anatomy that he knows. Unencumbered by the wisdom of history, by the techniques of painting, by all the vast armamentarium possessed by the lore master and the art critic, the surgeon is, perhaps, ill suited to a discussion of pictorial works. Still, with the same sweet arrogance of fools and children, let a surgeon presume to meditate.

In the beginning there was Leonardo da Vinci. Before him, the human body was seen in static terms, a piece of sculpture. Veiled as much by the taboo against dissection as by the integument that encased it, the interior of the body was terra incognita, an occult, untraveled place that lay hushed and kept its mystery. Around the turn of the sixteenth century, Leonardo, the inspired tinkerer, began the first of the thirty dissections he was to perform in his lifetime. Let us visit him in his prosectorium.

The bodies are lean. Leonardo insists on it: Excess of fat obscures the organs, prevents the fine definition of the fascicles of a muscle. There is also the problem of liquefaction in the Florentine heat. And so Leonardo must choose carefully. In this, he anticipates the surgeon, who, faced with the obesity of a patient, must shovel aside the masses of fat in which the arteries and nerves lie hidden like frightened lizards. No, the bodies must be lean. In leanness, too, there is that implication of strength and grace, a reminder of the much that was in the little that remains. But gaze long enough within these peeled and cored cadavers and slowly, imperceptibly, the organs take upon themselves a suffusion of ruddiness, subdued yet unmistakably there. Leonardo would try for that, varying the shade of brown ink, highlighting with white chalk. Gaze longer and the tissues swell. All at once the whole of the body seems invested with energy. He is coming to it—what he is seeking with all his heart—the soul that resides in a muscle, a brain, a spray of nerves. To find it he must fend off his repugnance for the handling, the odors. Worse still is the terror that attacks during the long candlelit nights spent in the company of flayed and shredded corpses.

Just see Leonardo, the huge, bearded man, hunched over a long table to which he himself has lifted the body. The back of a forearm has been slit, the outer layers peeled away. He rummages among the sinews, elevating one of them between thumb and forefinger into the opening he has made. It is a tendon into which all of the contractile power of a muscle is gathered and shot. Now he plucks it as though to extract music from it; the little finger of the cadaver lifts in a gesture of immense delicacy. He lets go of the cord and watches the little finger fall to its neutral position. Now he fishes in an incision he has made on the underside of the forearm, tugging first one, then another of the cords until he sees the little finger furl itself into the palm. Now he plays them both, tugging first one, then the other, and sees the marionette finger open and clench, open and clench, acting in accordance with the will of its master. Leonardo has found the *flexor digiti quinti*, and the *extensor digiti quinti proprius*. It is time to draw.

Leonardo did not always get it right. But he did get it righter by far than anyone before him or for thirty years afterward, when Vesalius would come along and found the science of anatomy. The stealthy Vesalius, who must also dissect in secret, scavenging for parts like a jackal beneath the gibbets of the newly hanged, then scurry to his dissecting room with a ghastly bulge beneath his cloak. By 1600, anatomy had become respectable. Daily, Julius Casserius demonstrated his dissections in Padua in an amphitheater crowded with students, dieners, curiosity seekers and assorted ghouls. Dogs prowled or lounged among the tables. In the gallery, rich women leaned above the hullabaloo holding vinegar-soaked handkerchiefs to their noses. Artists drew and etched on copper plates. The result, not published during Casserius's lifetime, was the *Tabulae Anatomicae, omnes novae nec ante hoc visae,* all new and never seen before.

If art be art only as it is informed with the principle of vitality, these copper plates fulfill the requirement. For here is a race of figures in a whole repertory of histrionic attitudes. We see the body uncensored by its integument and posed as in melodrama. The impulse is sensual, romantic. But unlike the *Laocöon,* whose facial agony and tortured extremities translate the suffering of the father and sons, these figures are strangely placid. They have endured; they have accepted. They are beyond pain. Stripped of the covering of their flesh, their souls are somehow visible.

Wearing their flayed skin like graceful drapery and set against strange, featureless landscapes, they are intent upon displaying themselves, posturing for the purposes of high pedagogy. Each of their gestures is a mixture of the wild and the delicate. What they are doing is *important:* It matters terribly to them that we behold their muscles, bones and viscera. It is as though they themselves are seeking to solve the mystery of their bodies, stripping down, peering within, only to find that the more of themselves they shed, the deeper the mystery becomes. For the body is but the side of the soul that faces outward. The onlooker gazes and gazes and at last is caught up in that mystery, not to solve, only to contemplate.

The placement of the seemingly unimportant details of anatomy is always at the center of attention. Still, these details, meant to serve the body, end in service to the spirit. How alone the creatures are, how silent, how deaf. With what submarine grace they model their flesh. Theirs is a kind of self-destructive heroism devoid of exhilaration or dejection and beyond deceit. For they are not symbols: They are what they are.

Here is a man with an acrobat's fatless grace, his arms and legs exhibiting a contrapuntal liveliness. He would have us see the muscles that hold up his head, but, distracted, we are drawn again and again to the bright globes of his buttocks. Another gropes to disentangle himself from the envelope of his skin, the better to be seen. Still another holds up the apron of his omentum to show us the root of his intestine. *Hinneni!* his face exclaims. Behold! Here am I. His flying fingers and bended knee, the very tilt of his head, hold him aloft. A pregnant woman literally blooms as she shows us the generative power of her womb. Through the opened petals of flesh, the eye of the viewer is riveted to the great abdominal event and her fecundity is proven. Look! her hair streams. Does a wind blow?

The walking pelvises—headless, truncated, with their solid netherworks have the dreamlike ambiguity of abstract art. In them, as in Picasso's work, integration is truly revealed by the process of disintegration. Earthbound, they are all beef and bone, meant, one thinks, to fetch and carry. Or are they extraterrestrial? Aliens working electronically? In any case, these do not chill our blood or horrify. We do not see ourselves in them. They are not of our species. It is the clinical gaze that is invited here.

In all of them the activity swirls in the tissues. The bodies themselves do the speaking. The faces, the poses, are static. There is no need to give each one a life history: This one was a mariner, that a tumbler. They are simply the essence of carnality. In the end, Casserius, having dissected their bodies to shreds, must leave his creatures to their silence. What these plates tell us is that there are mysteries beyond anything an anatomist can reveal with his scalpel, or an engraver with his stylus. And so from anatomy, that mutest of sciences, have come these mutes of art, lasting evidence of the restorative powers of the imagination.

Chapter 12

For each man and woman there is that building of childhood, the mere thought of which years later is enough to reawaken the whole of the buried past. For me it is the Gardner Earl Crematorium. Begun in 1887 and opened for use in 1902, the crematorium stands on a ridge overlooking the city of Troy. I first saw it in the company of Father. The year was 1936. Soon smoke from other crematoria would be drifting across Europe. But we could not know that. We had just left St. Mary's Hospital and, instead of turning toward home, Father pointed the old blue Hudson automobile north on Oakwood Avenue. It was October and we would, he proposed, go see the foliage.

"The Oakwood Cemetery is the best place for leaves," he said. "What with all those maples and oaks, the gravestones will be strewn with them." It is from Father that I inherited what

Mother called my "morbid strain." Just before the entrance to the cemetery and set back from the road was a stone building with a high tower at one end and a tall chimney at the other. The exterior of the building was of rough-hewn gray granite. The silhouette of the roof was broken by pinnacles and turrets. No garden surrounded it; no fountains splashed; no flags stirred. Only a single ancient oak, a Cerberus of a tree, full of gnarled vigor, that brooked no companions. Such a building is a shadow on a child's mind.

"What's that place?" I wanted to know. It could not have been built. It had to have fallen to earth with a terrible thud and squatted there ever since.

Father explained.

"It's the crematorium where the people who don't want to be buried are burned up in an oven. That"—he pointed—"is the chimney."

"Burned up? That's got to hurt."

"No it doesn't, silly boy. The dead don't feel pain. They are numb." He had a way of making a word like *numb* reverberate in your ear.

"But how do you know it doesn't hurt?"

"It just makes sense, that's all."

"But you can't prove it, can you?"

With a weary sigh: "No, I can't prove it, as I have never actually been dead. Only half, and that doesn't count."

"Just because we can't hear them hollering . . ."

"We'll go have a look at the leaves," said Father. I could tell that this outing had become his Delilah; already he regretted having lifted the corner of her tent. And well he might, if Mother ever found out where he had taken me, as concerned as she was about my dark cast of mind. But I would not be deterred.

"What happens to the smoke?"

"What do you mean what happens to the smoke? It goes up in the air."

"We breathe it in," I announced grimly.

"It's just particles of soot. After a while, it settles to the ground. Let's go look at the leaves."

"It comes down on our food and we eat it."

"The foliage," said Father, "now! And if I were you, I wouldn't mention any of this to your mother. Let it be our secret, yours and mine." Silence. "She is enough worried about you as it is." Silence. "Did you hear me?" Silence. "Do you want me to smack you with the hairbrush?" I broke the silence.

"You needn't worry, Father. I wouldn't dream of telling where you took me." There's nothing worse than a lofty child. At the cemetery we crunched through banks of autumn leaves. How they encrusted the gravestones, red and gold against the white marble.

"Where've you been?" said Billy, affecting indifference. He was as jealous as a cat.

"The crematorium," I replied. The word had been lying on the floor of my mouth. I gathered it up and hummed it at him.

"Crematorium?" said Billy. "What's that?" I told him. "Judas Priest!" he said. The next day after school we walked up to see it.

"It looks like a dragon," said Billy. And so it did! What with its low squat body, the high tower topped by a narrow head, and that rigid tail of a chimney. Even as he spoke, I imagined its horrid feasting, the belching of smoke. All afternoon Billy and I prowled around the building, waiting for something to happen, a revelation that would split open the barriers to the supernatural. There w.s no sign of life, either inside or out. Still, we had the feeling that we were being watched. It was the dragon itself keeping us in view. All the windows save the two nearest the chimney were of stained glass. You couldn't see through them. Ever since, I have thought the real purpose of stained glass is not decoration but to keep you from seeing what's on the other side. Through the clear windows at the back, by jumping up and down, we could just make out the corner of a pale-green metal box with a row of rivets along the edge.

"The oven!" we exclaimed with a blend of dread and ecstasy. Hours passed while Billy and I scared ourselves to death with eerie moans and shrieks of demonic laughter, casting over-the-shoulder glances to see if the dragon had lashed its tail. Not Thomas Gray and forty country churchyards could have elicited so many shivers. Only missing was the moping owl.

It was the unbreakable rule at our house that children must not be late for meals. Supper was served promptly at six o'clock. You came late to the table, you went without. But, unbeknownst to us, night had fallen. A mass of dark clouds had muscled across the Hudson Valley. You couldn't see the sky. All at once, the clouds parted to reveal the tower of the crematorium blowing a slender upraised bugle of moon. At that precise moment a sharp blare of thunder sounded overhead. We jumped right out of the United States. Just as swiftly, the clouds closed. Had we seen the dragon reach up and tear that moon from the sky, we could not have been rendered more lunatic.

Fate, take over! I thought. And so she did. A dark figure stepped from behind the oak tree where it had been lurking, its hideous intention, I knew, bent upon us. In a moment we would be seized by the evil caretaker of the place and flung into his oven. But it was no such thing. It was Father, coming toward us in his long overcoat and fedora. The sight of the glowing tip of his Lucky Strike was Balm in Gilead. Dizzy with relief, I ran toward him, only to stop just out of arm's reach at a glimpse of his countenance. With a jolt of terrestrial fear, I realized that we had missed supper. It would not go well with us. Holding each of us by an ear, Father marched to the car and tossed us into the backseat.

"We lost track of the time," said Billy. A craven speech that was greeted with the wordless contempt it so richly deserved. The rest of the ride home was made in silence. No sooner were we inside the door than Father pointed his marching finger upstairs to the room Billy and I shared and where all our anguished paraphernalia had flung itself about in sympathy. From the mantel Father took down the silver-plated hairbrush. Nor spake he a single word. None was needed. The firmness with which he closed his grip about the handle was eloquence enough. What a hypocritical thing is a hairbrush that puts itself forward as an article for grooming but is, in fact, a bastinado. *Potch! Potch! Potch! Potch!*

When the storm had passed, the netherlands of Troy were on fire. Never mind. It was worth it. For now, Billy and I had in our hearts the very architecture of death. In the months to come, there and there alone would dwell imagination. It would dream of nothing else. Besides, we had paid dearly for that crematorium. What comes dearly is dearly held.

Weeks later, pedaling up Oakwood Avenue alone, I saw a row of cars pull up in front of the crematorium.

The first in line was a hearse. I raced to catch up, threw down my bike and ran to hide behind the guardian oak. A small knot of mourners followed the coffin into the building. When I heard the door click shut, I tiptoed to the window, through which I could see the corner of the oven. Minutes went by. The air trembled with premonition. Looking up, I saw issuing from the chimney a thin strand of grayish smoke. It turned slowly in the air like a shroud unwinding, a shroud that kept for a long moment the shape of the human being it had lately enfolded before fanning out over the ridge. That same year I had been reading Dickens—about boys my age who crawled into chimneys to scrape away the soot. Breathed there a sweep so brave as to clean this one? I could not imagine it.

At the turn of the century the population of Troy was almost entirely Irish Catholic. In that faith, cremation was widely held to be repugnant, if not barbarian. It was also an impediment to the resurrection of the flesh. Had there been Jews or Muslims, they would have felt the same way. Most of the crematorium's clients were Protestants from out of town. Any day of the week but Sunday, one of them might arrive on the morning train from New York City. In each party, an extra ticket had been purchased for the body, which was transported as freight. The Union Depot was on Sixth Avenue, one block from where I lived. How often I have imagined it:

Four black-suited men in top hats lower the coffin from a freight car and load it onto a black horse-drawn hearse that is draped in each corner with purple. The heads of the horses are topped with black ostrich plumes; their bellies are tied about with sashes of crepe. Torches blaze from silver fixtures at the sides of the carriage. There is the muffled solemnity of drums. Other carriages wait for those mourners who cannot manage the steep climb to the cemetery. The rest trail after on foot. The horses turn toward Hoosick Street, stepping slowly, not trotting but in mournful cadence. All along the route, some two miles, citizens halt as the cortege passes by. No man but removes his cap; no woman but crosses herself and moves her lips in whispers for the repose of the defunct.

Time and again during the fifty years that have passed, I have dispatched my dreaming mind to that ridge overlooking the Hudson River, to that building whose spell, cast over me in childhood, has never been lifted. At last the day has come when I have left the armchair in the little study in New Haven where I read and write, and I have returned to Troy to confront the crematorium.

I'm standing at the gates to the Oakwood Cemetery. To my left the crematorium is comprised of equal parts of light and shadow. I see that the oak tree is no more. Nor is there any sign of a stump. When had it wrenched up its arthritic roots and limped off? Instead, there is a lawn civilized with precisely clipped evergreen shrubs. It is noon, but not even the noonday sun reveals this place. Rather, it is the visitor who is revealed to the building. It knows my fate. Standing before it, I am aware of my sixty years, my gray hair, "the wormy circumstance" of my clothes. Here is a building that has the appearance of having been built yesterday. A hundred years of rain and wind have made no mark upon it. It is as it was at the beginning, a building that had no infancy, had no ripening to do, but was from the moment of its construction fully adult. It is impossible not to think of an animal, a frozen mammoth in Siberia or a creature that has crawled up from deep beneath the ground and that sleeps and sleeps until, stirred by hunger, it awakens with a fire in its belly.

Arrangements have been made and I am to be guided by the caretaker, who is walking toward me, keys in hand. A more unlikely Charon could not be imagined. Tom Gibson is thirty-one, short, pigeon plump, with a blond beard, Irish good looks and a welcoming smile. He wears a baseball cap and a jacket with the words NEW YORK GIANTS on the back. In his running shoes he is a muscular, soft-footed cat. Together we walk the perimeter of the crematorium. The building faces the east, from which it receives the first rays of the rising sun. It is one hundred and forty-six feet in length and, at its widest, seventy-five. The chapel and its tower are connected by loggia comprised of three massive arches. From the northernmost roof rises the tall slender chimney, flared gracefully at the top. The square tower is eighteen feet around and ninety feet high. Seventy feet up is a balcony. Above this is the belfry, which is open on all four sides. Between the tower and the chimney lies a profusion of turrets, pinnacles and gables. No longer of slate, the roof is now of molded copper. The impression is not at all that of a church. It is, instead, a sarcophagus, which, as the ancient Greeks believed, ate the flesh placed within it, leaving behind the indigestible bones. The walls, tower and chimney, all in gray granite, suggest secrecy, as though a gray cloak has been thrown over the interior. Overlooking the Hudson River Valley, the crematorium suggests the patience of the immortal that waits for the inconsequential to get itself over with.

At the rear of the building, a tame garage lies tethered. Through its open door, I see a backhoe, a squadron of lawnmowers, tree saws, picks and shovels. The caretaker explains that he and his two helpers must, in addition to their crematorium duties, mow the grass in the cemetery, prune dead branches, dig the graves, lower the coffins, replace the earth, set the stones.

"That's a lot of work," I tell him.

"Yeah? You think so? Well there ain't any hurry. What don't get done, waits." Together the caretaker and I mount the steps to the loggia. Passing beneath an arch changes one so. On the other side is always an altogether different do-

main entered with trepidation and expectancy.
Anything might happen there. Tom Gibson unlocks the door to the tower at the southern end
of the loggia. He leads the way as we climb a
marble-and-wrought-iron spiral staircase to a
landing. A second spiral staircase brings us to the
base of an iron ladder, which we ascend hand
over hand to the belfry. There is no longer a
bell. In its place, swarming from a hive in the
eaves, a thousand bees offer their bronze hum so
that the air vibrates as after a gong has been
struck. The caretaker, wary of them, pulls at his
cap. If the chimney is the tail of the beast, this
belfry is its eye. Far below us stretches the whole
of the valley. I see the confluence of the Mohawk
and the Hudson rivers, the Cohoes Falls, the
towns that line either bank—Cohoes, Watervliet
and Troy itself. At our feet, the copper sheets of
the roof gleam. Yes! Like the scales of a dragon.

When I have seen enough, Tom leads the
way down and unlocks the door to the chapel.
Here he stands aside to let me enter. With that
first glance, I have the sense that I have seen this
room before. But where? In a former life, perhaps. Or had it until now remained, like Psyche's
grotto, an untrodden chamber of my mind? Immediately upon crossing the threshold, I am not
in a building at all but aboard a yacht whose
wardrooms and cabins are fitted out with every
sumptuous furnishing, each meant to divert the
passengers' attention from the pitching seas all
around. The ceiling of the chapel is of quartered
oak with intricate open timberwork. The chairs
and benches are of the same wood. The floor is
of bluestone. There are four large Tiffany

stained-glass windows—ruby and dark blue with greenish lights. The walls and all the fixtures are of red-and-black marble.

The reception room is even more clamorous, with pillars of green onyx, blind arcades, bronze doors and walls of pink-and-gray marble. No use to listen for a still, small voice above this din. Try as they might, these furnishings do not deceive. Each bit of decor by itself is beautiful. Taken together they give off a faint, sickish vulgarity. It is a place you inhabit in a claustrophobic nightmare from which you awaken terrified and gasping. All the powers of sensory persuasion cannot distract the thoughts from that box full of fire.

It is evening. I have said goodnight to the caretaker and we have arranged to meet tomorrow at noon. Perhaps I should not have come here in March, when the light is pale and troubled. March is what is left of winter; it is winter hanging by a thread.

It is the next day, and I am to witness a cremation. At precisely three-thirty, a hearse arrives and backs up to the entrance of the retort room. In the hearse are three long flat cardboard boxes, each one labeled. The word HEAD is printed at one end of each box. Tom and his helpers, Rich and Lou, slide the boxes onto waist-high carts fitted out with rollers. Papers of identification and receipt are checked and signed. The hearse departs. Tom presses the button that raises the doors of the ovens. They are lined with firebrick. In each, a trough runs partly down the middle of the floor. The men slide the boxes one by one from the carts, each into its own oven. Buttons are pressed; the doors are lowered.

"I'll show you how it works," says Tom. Watching this caretaker at his valves and buttons, I think again of Father. I see him ceremonially rolling up his shirt sleeves, then kneeling into the fireplace to set the kindling, holding each log gently and with respect in his beautiful priest's hands.

"You have to set one next to the other just so," he would say. "They've got to touch in order for the fire to pass back and forth between them. Be sure to leave room for air so that the first little flame can breathe." He might have been instructing us in the act of love. Moments later—it never failed—a blaze, and his tiny smile of pride and pleasure. At intervals, Mother, with a kerchief over her hair, collected the ashes and sprinkled them on her house plants.

"There's nothing like ashes to make the begonias grow," she'd say.

No one else was permitted to set and light a fire at our house. Once, like Prometheus, I stole a box of kitchen matches and Billy and I set fire to some old crates in the empty lot at the back of the house. It says something about the impoverishment of the modern imagination that, while Prometheus's punishment for the same crime was to be chained to a rock and have his liver pecked out by an eagle, Billy and I suffered only the same old hairbrush used for any mundane infraction. Not until I was thirteen and Father had died did I make a fire in the hearth. It was a short-lived smoky affair that told me point blank that I wasn't ready yet. Ever since, the most cheerful blaze in a fireplace contains for me one ember of that old sorrow. From Father I learned that fire ends life, then sets it forth into a new existence. In the heart of the fire, death is no longer death; it has been annulled by the flames. And here, in this crematorium, is the crucible where the transformation is enacted.

"The head and the heart take the longest time to burn up," says Tom. "Arms and legs don't need more than an hour. The hottest place is closer to the door. That's why they got to go in feet first. We give it three hours anyway at fourteen hundred degrees Fahrenheit, just to be sure." He presses the starter buttons and blowers, and sets the automatic shut-off. Rich and Lou get in an old red truck labeled TROY CEMETERY ASSOCIATION and go off for coffee.

"I'll show you where we keep the remains," says Tom. We climb a flight of stairs to a room lined with shelves laden with urns of ashes, bouquets of artificial flowers and photographs of the dead.

"I wouldn't want to be put here," I tell him.

"You wouldn't?"

"No, I'd rather be scattered somewhere." It is the one preference I am sure of.

"We've got bags and bags of ashes in the basement. Nobody even knows who they are."

Rich and Lou have come back with the coffee. They toot for us to come and get it. The four of us stand around outside drinking and smoking cigarettes. Above, flames are shooting out of the chimney.

"Okay," says Tom. "Now I'll give you a look

inside. It's been on for half an hour." He presses the OPEN button. The door rises and a blast of heat slaps my face. The smell of meat roasting seeks out my mouth, fills the back of my throat. There is the sound of spitting and of the flames rolling their R's. Inside, the corpse is animated, the head thrown back so that the face is visible, the mouth darkly agape, lips shrunk to the gums. The bosses of the skull are bright as butter in the firelight. And as yellow. The arms, which had been at the sides, are lifted as if to fend something off. As I watch, there is a slow washing movement of the hands. In the trough below, a liquid bubbling.

"The lady wasn't embalmed," says the caretaker. He points to the trough. "Those are the body fluids."

"How do you know that?" I ask him.

"How do I know what?"

"That it's a . . . a . . . lady?" The word is uneasy in my mouth.

"Oh, I can tell all right. I can tell." At that moment, it might have been Father shaking his head sadly. "So," he would be saying, "you have learned nothing. Fifty years ago you gave back to the dead the curse of sensation. And still you do."

"No, no," I whisper to his shade. "The dead lose all reticence and speak more freely than the living."

"You!" I hear him give a deep sigh of damnation. "You'll never grow up."

I am aware that the three—Tom, Rich and Lou—are watching me. There is mischief in their smiles, the way they glance at one another, hu-

mor overflowing their eyes. They are boys, playing navy, floating their ships in the pond, then
setting them on fire. All three are immensely
proud of their work, and lighthearted, peppy as
though refreshed by the presence of death. I
have none of their sangfroid. Above the voices
of the oven, it is Tom's voice that leads me by
the hand.

"It's somethin' you don't take personally," he
says. The others nod. "It don't bother me none.
I even had two of my best buddies in here. Slid
'em right on in and turned on the gas myself. I
was glad I could do it for 'em."

I see that these men have moved beyond the
horrific, where I am trapped. It is not that their
imaginations have been blunted; it is that mine
is overheated. That "morbid" cast of mind. Tom
closes the oven door. All that remains of that
hellfire lies in my eyes. We shake hands and plan
to meet again in the morning. Outside, rain is
falling. Troy is filled with its green fragrance.

When I arrive, the ovens have been swept
out. A frost of ashes clings to the firebrick, as
though not heat but cold had raged there. Rich
is carrying a bin of cinders to a stone table.
Among them lie fragments of bone an inch or
more in length. Here and there I recognize a
ridge or a groove where once a muscle arose or
inserted. It is Rich's job to pound them into
ashes. With each blow of his hammer, a small
cloud of bone dust rises. His hands are white
with it. His face, too. When he has finished, he
scoops the ashes into an urn and labels it. Then
on to the next.

"We do five hundred a year," says Tom. "You got any questions?"

"How much does it cost?" It is all I can think to ask.

"Only one hundred and thirty dollars."

"That *is* cheap."

Tom turns to Rich. "We gonna lift tonight?"

"Yeah."

"Lift?" I say.

Tom explains. "Me and Rich lift weights sometimes after work."

It is the fourth day of my visit. The caretaker has brought me as far as he can. For the remainder of my stay he has lent me a key to the crematorium. I am to come and go as I please. The weather has turned cold. It has snowed, melted, frozen. The north side of the belfry shows fangs of ice. At the hotel, they have lit a fire in the tavern. I sit facing it. Each time I raise my glass, it fills with feathered orange, until what I am drinking is fire.

Day after day I roam the languid undulations of the cemetery hills or go to sit alone in the raftered gallery. With each hour the impulse to scoff at what I had first seen as sentimental clichés of the hereafter grows dimmer. What had seemed a duplicity of furnishings has become a purity of intention. I see it in the reddish marble whose arterial tracery streams with golden corpuscles. I see it in the gules—blood and grape—transmitted through the stained glass as the sun moves across the sky. How they tremble on the walls, the floor, quickening the dark skeleton of oaken ribs, taking the gloom.

They were honest masons who made this place a hundred years ago, they who had hewed and carved, etched and polished, fashioning their version of paradise out of a passion for their trowels and chisels. Perhaps those men had no conception of art; perhaps they were untouched by learning. It doesn't matter. The work of their hands had a holiness of its own, and to those whose sensibilities have not been dulled by excessive intellect or cynicism, the holiness is still there a century later.

It is time to leave the dew-struck hills of Troy and return to the round of my life. In the week since I arrived, I have gazed and gazed. And gazed myself out. The crematorium has spoken, yielding up its secret and instructing me how to live. Or rather, how to die. Minutes ago, I signed a form "solemnly expressing" to my next of kin my wish to be cremated in this building when the time comes. In the place where it called for a witness, Tom Gibson wrote his name. He walks me to my car.

"Tom," I say. "What's your idea of the hereafter? Or is it all just a box of ashes so far as you're concerned?"

"The next life?" He smiles, shrugs. "About that I wouldn't want to say." He looks off into the distance. "Sometimes I watch those flames shooting out of the chimney and I wonder."

I go to open the car door. But I don't yet. On the door handle, a butterfly. Come so early! It is black, edged with sulfur. Slowly, the upright wings open and close. I feel the pulse captive in them. The soft valvular systole. Diastole.

Chapter 13

A little more than a year ago, I received a phone call from a poet I knew slightly. Would I, he wondered, be willing to intervene in behalf of a friend of his who was dying of AIDS?

"Intervene?"

"His suffering is worthy of Job. He wants to commit suicide while he still has the strength to do it."

"Do you know what you are asking?"

"I know, I know."

"No," I told him. "I am trained to preserve life, not end it. It is not in me to do a thing like that."

"Then I am to assume that one function of a doctor is to prolong a misfortune as long as possible?"

"There is society," I replied. "There is the law. I am not a barbarian who lives outside the precincts of society and the law."

"You are precisely that," he says. "A barbarian."

"But why are you calling *me*?"

"I've read your books. It occurred to me that you might just be the right one."

I let the poet know that I had retired from medicine five years before, that I was no longer a doctor.

"Once a doctor, always a doctor," he replied. What I did not tell him was that I have continued to renew my license to prescribe narcotics each year. You never know . . . Someday I might have need of it to relieve pain or to kill myself easily should the occasion arise. If for myself, then why not for another?

"I'll think about it," I said. He gave me the patient's address and phone number.

"I implore you," said the poet. The conversation shifted to the abominable gymnastics of writing, a little gossip. We hung up. *Don't!* I told myself.

January 14, 1990

They live on the seventh floor of an apartment building about a ten-minute walk from my house. The doorman on duty is a former patient of mine. He greets me warmly, lifts his shirt to show me his gallbladder incision, how well it has healed.

"You can hardly see it," he says. That is the sort of thing that happens when I leave my study and reenter the world. The doorman lets me in. At precisely 4 P.M., as arranged, I knock on the door. It is opened by . . . let him be Lionel, a handsome man in his late thirties. We recognize each other as presences on the campus of the university. He is an ordained minister. He tells me that he has made use of my writings in his sermons. In the living room Ramon is sitting in an invalid's cushion on the sofa. A short, delicate man, also in his thirties. Ramon is a doctor specializing in public health—women's problems, birth control, family planning, AIDS. He is surprisingly unwasted, although pale as a blank sheet of paper. He gives me a brilliant smile around even, white teeth. The eyes do not participate in the smile. He and Lionel have been lovers for six years.

Ramon's hair is close-cropped, black; there is a neat lawn of beard. He makes a gesture as if to stand, but I stop him. His handshake is warm and dry and strong. There is a plate of chocolate-chip cookies on a table. Lionel pours tea. Lionel's speech is clipped, slightly mannered. Ramon has a Spanish accent; he is Colombian. For a few minutes we step warily around the reason I have come there. All at once, we are engaged. I ask him about his symptoms. He tells me of his profound fatigue, the mental depression, the intractable diarrhea, his ulcerated hemorrhoids. He has Kaposi's sarcoma. Only yesterday a new lesion appeared in the left naso-orbital region. He points to it. Through his beard I see another, larger black tumor. His mouth is dry, encrusted from the dehydration. He clutches his abdomen, grimaces. There is the odor of stool.

"I want to die," he announces calmly, without the least emotion.

"Is it so bad?"

"Yes, it is."

"But how can I be sure? On Tuesday, you want to die; by Thursday, perhaps you will have changed your mind." He nods to Lionel, who helps him to stand. The three of us go into their bedroom, where Ramon lies on his side and offers his lesions as evidence. I see that his anus is a great circular ulceration, raw and oozing blood. His buttocks are smeared with pus and liquid stool. With tenderness, Lionel bathes and dresses him in a fresh diaper. Although I have been summoned here, I feel very much the intruder upon their privacy. And I am convinced.

We return to the living room. Lionel and Ramon sit side by side on the sofa, holding hands. A lethal dose of barbiturates is en route from a doctor friend in Colombia. Ramon wants to be certain that it will not fail. He wants, too, that Lionel be with him, holding him, and that Lionel not cry. He couldn't bear that, he says. Lionel says that of course he will cry, that he must be allowed to. Lionel is afraid that it might not work, that he will be discovered as an accomplice.

"I am the sole beneficiary of the will," he explains. Lionel does not want to be alone when the time comes. He has never seen anyone die before. A minister? Has he never attended a deathbed?

"It's just worked out that way," he says. "I'm a teacher." Still, I am shocked at such a state of virginity. We have a discussion. It is about death as best friend, not enemy. How sensible the pagans are, for whom death is a reunion with the spirit world that resides in nature. While one member of the tribe returns to nature, the tribe lives on. It is a far cry from the Christian concept of death and resurrection. Ramon's vision is failing; soon he will be blind. He coughs, shifts on the pillow, swallows a pain pill. He tells me that he has taken all of the various experimental medicines without relief from the diarrhea. His entire day is spent dosing himself and dealing with the incontinence. Despite chemotherapy, the tumors are growing rapidly. His palate is covered with them. He opens his mouth for me to see. Above all, he wants to retain his dignity, to keep control of his life, which he equates with choosing the time and method of suicide. Soon he will be unable to do it.

"But death," I say. "It is so final."

"I want it," he says again, on his face a look of longing. He wants me to obtain the injectable narcotics that would ensure death, if needed. I offer to return in a few days to talk. Ramon urges me to think of myself as merely an instrument that he will take up to rescue himself. An instrument? But I am a man.

The tone turns conspiratorial. Our voices drop. We admonish each other to be secretive, tell no one. There are those who would leap to punish. I suggest that he arrange for a codicil to his will requesting that there be no autopsy.

January 16

My second visit. Four in the afternoon. Ramon answers the door. He has lost ground. His eyes are sunken, his gait tottering. He is in great pain, which he makes no effort to conceal. As arranged, he is alone. Lionel is to return in an hour. The barbiturates have arrived from Colombia. He shows me the bottles of tablets in the bottom drawer of the dresser. A quick calculation informs me that he has well over the lethal dose. The diarrhea has been unrelenting. The Kaposi's sarcoma is fulminating, with new lesions every day.

"I have always counted so much on my looks," he says shyly and without the least immodesty. "What if I vomit the pills?" I tell him to take them at a regular pace, each with only a sip of water so as not to fill up too quickly. If it is necessary, would I inject more medication? "I have good veins," he says, rolling up a sleeve. I see that he does. There are several puncture marks at the antecubital fossa, where blood had been drawn. One more would not be noticed.

"When?" I ask him.

"No later than one month." Did I want to choose a date? He rises with difficulty, gets a calendar from the kitchen. We bend over it. "Are you free on February tenth? It is a Saturday."

"I am free." February 10! There is a date!

I ask about his life. He was born and raised in Medellín, one of four sisters and three brothers. His mother had no formal education but she is "very wise." It is clear that he loves her. No, she knows nothing; not that he is gay nor that he is ill. He has written a letter to be sent postmortem, telling her that he loves her, thanking her for all that she has done. In the family, only an older brother knows, and to him it is a disgrace. He has forbidden Ramon to tell the others. His four sisters live near his mother in Medellín.

There are twelve grandchildren. His mother will not be alone. (He smiles at this.) Had he always known he was gay? He discovered his attraction to men at age eight, but of course it was impossible to express it. Colombia is a macho country. At seventeen, he went to Bogotá to study medicine. For six years he lived in an apartment with four other Medellín boys. There was much camaraderie but no sexual expression. It was a "quiet" student's life. After one year of internship in a hospital, he decided against clinical medicine. It was while working toward a degree in public health at Yale that he met Lionel. The year was 1983. After he completed his studies, he and Lionel were separated for two years, although they visited each other frequently. There followed a three-year period when they lived together in New Haven. Shortly after they met, Ramon began to feel ill. He told Lionel at once and they agreed to discontinue sex. Aside from mutual caressing, there has been no sexual contact between them since.

"It was not sex that brought us together," Ramon says. "It was love." I lower my gaze, I who have always hesitated before expressing love.

Lionel returns. It is the first day of the semester at Yale. A day of meeting with students, advising, counseling. He is impeccably dressed. He is accompanied by a woman, someone I know slightly. He notices my surprise.

"This is Melanie," he announces. "She is all right." He places his arm about her waist. "She is the sister I have always wanted."

Lionel bends to kiss Ramon on the cheek. "*Chiquito!* You are wearing your new shirt."

I am alarmed by the presence of the woman, Melanie. It is clear that she knows everything. We sit around the table drinking tea.

"Tell me about death," says Lionel.

"What do you mean?"

"The details. You're a doctor—you should know. What about the death rattle?"

"It has been called that." I explain about not being able to clear secretions from the lungs.

"What sort of equipment will we need?"

"Nothing. You already have the diapers."

"Ramon has to die in diapers?" I explain about the relaxation of the bowel and urinary sphincters, that it would be best.

"I shouldn't have asked." Lionel seems increasingly nervous. "I'm terrified of the police," he says. "I always have been. Should I see a lawyer? What if I'm caught and put in prison?" He begins to weep openly. "And I am losing Ramon. That is a fact, and there is not a thing I can do about it!" When he continues to cry without covering his face, Ramon reaches out a hand to console him.

"Look," I say. "You are not ready for this and, to tell the truth, I'm not sure I am either."

"Oh, please!" Ramon's voice is a high-pitched plea of distress. "It is only a matter of a few minutes of misery. I would be dying anyway after that." Lionel pulls himself together, nods to show that he understands. I begin to feel that my presence is putting pressure on Lionel, that my being there makes it real, imminent. I tell him that I am ready to withdraw. How easy that would be. A way out.

"You are the answer to Ramon's prayers," Lionel says. "To him you are an angel." But to

Lionel I am the angel of death. "And, of course, I agree to whatever Ramon wants to do."

It is Ramon who turns practical. "If it is too hard for you, Lionel, I won't mind if you are not here with me." And to me: "Lionel simply cannot lie. If questioned by the police, he would have to tell the truth." I see that the lying will be up to me. Throughout, Melanie has remained silent.

We go through the "script," Lionel's word. In the bedroom, Ramon will begin taking the pills. I will help him. Lionel and Melanie will wait in the living room.

Lionel: "Will we be in the apartment all the time until he dies?"

Melanie speaks for the first time: "Not necessary. We can go out somewhere and return to find him dead."

Lionel: "Where would we go?"

Melanie: "Anywhere. For a walk; to the movies."

Lionel: "How long will it take?"

Me: "Perhaps all day."

Lionel: "What if the doctors notify the police? Ramon has made no secret of his intentions at the clinic. They have even withheld pain medication because he is 'high risk.'" I tell Ramon that on his next visit to the clinic, he is to ask for a prescription for fifty Levo-Dromoran tablets. Maybe they will give him that many. Maybe not.

Lionel: "I simply can't believe they would turn us in, but there's no way to be sure, is there?" More and more we are like criminals, or a cell of revolutionaries. Lionel's fear and guilt are infectious. But then there is Ramon. I stand up to leave, assuring them that I will come again on Sunday at four in the afternoon. Melanie says that she will be there too. Lionel hopes he has not shaken my resolve. He apologizes for his weakness.

"We'll talk further," I say. Ramon takes my hand.

"You have become my friend. In such a short time. One of the best friends of my life."

The next day there is a note from Lionel in his small, neat handwriting. He thanks me. Enclosed is a copy of a lecture he had given in 1984 in which he cited an incident from one of my books, about a doctor who stays his hand out of mercy. It is strangely prophetic and appropriate to the circumstances. My nights are ridden with fantasies: I am in the bedroom with Ramon. We are sitting side by side on the bed. He is wearing only a large blue disposable diaper. The bottles of pills are on the nightstand, along with a pitcher of water and a glass. Ramon pours a handful of the tiny tablets into his palm, then, with a shy smile, begins to swallow them one at a time. Because of the dryness of his mouth and the fungal infection of his throat, it is painful. And slow.

"You are drinking too much water," I say. "You will fill up too quickly."

"I will try," he says. What seems like hours go by. From the living room comes the sound of Mozart's clarinet quintet. Ramon labors on, panting, coughing. When he has finished one bottle, I open another. His head and arms begin to wobble. I help him to lie down.

"Quickly," I tell him. "We don't have much time left." I hold the glass for him, guide it to his lips. He coughs, spits out the pills.

"Hold me," he says. I bend above him, cradle his head in my arm.

"Let yourself go," I say. He does, and minutes later he is asleep. I free myself and count the pills that are left, calculate the milligrams. Not enough. It is too far below the lethal dose. I take a vial of morphine and a syringe from my pocket, a rubber tourniquet. I draw up ten cubic centimeters of the fluid and inject it into a vein in Ramon's arm. The respirations slow down at once. I palpate his pulse. It wavers, falters, stops. There is a last long sigh from the pillow.

All at once, a key turns in the door to the bedroom. The door is flung open. Two men in fedoras and raincoats enter the bedroom. They are followed by the doorman whose gallbladder I had removed.

"You are under arrest," one of them announces.

"What is the charge?" I ask, clinging to a pretense of innocence.

"For the murder of Ramon Chavez."

I am startled by the mention of his last name. Had I known it? I am led away.

January 26

Melanie, Lionel, Ramon and me. Ramon's smile of welcome plays havoc with my heart. It is easy to see why Lionel fell in love with him. I offer an alternative: Ramon could simply stop eating and drinking. It would not take too many days. For some reason, both Lionel and Ramon cannot accept this. Lionel cannot watch him die of thirst. There is a new black tumor on Ramon's upper lip. He has visited the clinic, obtained thirty Levo-Dromoran tablets. I must test him again.

Me: "I think you are not ready. February tenth is too soon."

Ramon (covering his face with his hands, moaning): "Why do you say I am not ready?"

Me: "Because you have not done it already. Because you have chosen a method that is not certain, because you are worrying about Lionel."

Lionel: "I feel that I am an obstruction."

Me: "No, only that you are unreliable. You cannot tell the lies that may be necessary."

Lionel: "I'm sorry, I'm sorry."

Me: "Don't apologize for virtue. It doesn't make sense."

Ramon: "There is one thing. I prefer to do it at night, after dark. It would be easier for me." That, if nothing else, is comprehensible. Youth bids farewell to the moon more readily than to the sun.

We rehearse the revised plan. Lionel, Melanie and Ramon will dine together, "love each other," say good-bye. Lionel and Melanie will take the train to New York for the night. At 6 P.M. Ramon will begin to swallow the pills. At half past eight I will let myself into the apartment. The doorman may or may not question me, but I shall have a key. I am to stay only long enough to ensure that Ramon is dead. If he is not, I shall use the morphine; if he is, I shall not notify anyone. At noon the next day, Lionel and Melanie will return, discover the body and call the clinic. It is most likely that a doctor will come to pronounce death. Of course, he will ask questions, perhaps notice something, demand an autopsy. In which case, Lionel will show him the codicil to the will that requests that no autopsy be performed. Melanie questions whether that is binding. We are all clearly exhausted at the end of the session.

February 3

Saturday afternoon. It is to be our final visit. Ramon is worried that because of the diarrhea he will not absorb the barbiturate. He has seen undigested potassium tablets in his stool. I tell him not to worry; I will make sure. His gratitude is infinitely touching, infinitely sad. We count the pills. There are 110 of them, totaling eleven grams. The lethal dose is four and a half grams. Plus the remaining Levo-Dromoran. I have already obtained the vial of morphine and the syringe. Ramon is bent, tormented, but smiles when I hug him good-bye.

"I'll see you on Saturday," I tell him.

"But I won't see you," he replies with his shy smile. On the elevator, I utter aloud a prayer that I will not have to use the morphine.

February 7

Lunch at a restaurant with Lionel and Melanie.

"It's no good," says Melanie. "You're going to get caught."

"What makes you think so?" I ask.

"Why would a doctor with a practice of one patient be present at a known suicide-oriented patient's death?" She has talked with the Hemlock Society, with a sympathetic lawyer. There is no way to prevent an autopsy. By Connecticut law, the newly dead must lie in the funeral parlor for forty-eight hours. The coroner will see the body. Because of Ramon's youth and the suspicion of suicide, he will order an autopsy. Any injected substance would be discovered. The time of death can be estimated with some accuracy. I would have been seen entering the building around that time. The police would ask questions. Interviewed separately, Lionel, Melanie and I would give varying answers. It would be I who would be named. There would be the publicity, the press. It would be vicious. "No, you are fired, and that's that." I long to give in to the wave of relief that sweeps over me. But there is Ramon.

"What about Ramon and my promise?"

"We just won't tell him that you are not coming."

"The coward's way," I say.

"That is what we are, isn't it?"

February 11

A phone call from Lionel. Ramon is "very much alive." He is at the hospital, in the intensive-care unit. They have put him on the respirator, washed out his stomach. He is being fed by vein.

"I had to call the ambulance, didn't I?" Lionel asks. "What else could I do? He was alive."

February 15

I am at the bedside in the intensive-care unit. Ramon is still on the respirator, but he has regained consciousness. When he opens his eyes and sees me, there is a look on his face that I can only interpret as reproach and disappointment. He knows that I was not there. Lionel, the honest, has told him.

"Do you want to be treated for the pneumonia?" I ask. Ramon nods. "Do you want to live?" Ramon nods. "Do you want to die?" Ramon shakes his head.

It took him twelve days to die.

March 1

Lionel and I meet on the street. We are shy, embarrassed, like two people who share a shameful secret.

"We must get together soon," says Lionel.

"By all means. We should talk." We never do.

Chapter 14

Once again I have returned to Troy. For three days I have stitched up the old lacerated streets with my footsteps, gathering in my harvest of thorns. In Washington Park I come upon a small crop of cobblestones exactly like potatoes, all but covered with earth. I uncover them with my shoe and gaze until my eyes have had their fill of them. I see that a great effort has been made to restore the center of town. All the signs have been painted black with gold lettering. The brick façades have been pointed up and painted. Trees have been planted. Troy has become picturesque. There is no longer the night train to Montreal. The tracks have been removed, the railroad station torn down. What, I wonder, do the people do without the train whistle and the clackety wheels to induce sleep? Where once there was a row of brothels, there is now a bank. In the bar of the Hendrik Hudson Hotel there is no sawdust strewn upon the floor, not a single cuspidor. Men and women in shorts and running shoes are drinking Perrier. No one is smoking. The atmosphere is restrained. The long-stemmed glassware in the overhead rack seems to demand good deportment. No one is singing. What a far cry from my boisterous Central Tavern, where everyone was loyal to his five senses, and Duffy's malarkey came up like foam in a glass of Genesee beer, where eating a hard-boiled egg was not a venial sin and salvation was not the same as longevity.

Efforts at gentrification aside, Troy still strikes a faint note of Depression-era despondency, as though everyone in the town were living down some ancient misfortune. Precisely because it was bereft, pigeon-colored, in despair, I loved Troy. Tidier now, lacking in municipal pathos, respectable, the heroic imagination is nowhere visible. Can it be that, like Ishmael, I alone am left to tell how it used to be? Well, the bells of the churches are dead. The air no longer smells of soot. Only the light on the walls is the same, and the *tump-tump* of the river pounding the wharf. In a drugstore on River Street an old man accosts me.

"You," he says, a note of accusation in his voice. "Ain't you Dickie, the doctor's boy?"

"I was once," I tell him. "Perhaps I can be again."

Evening. Little by little Troy disengages itself from the sun and drops its colors, turning all the pale Irish as gold as Rembrandt's Jews.

How quiet it is.

It takes the silence of a town like Troy to stir

the mind. I walk from the hotel to the block of
Fifth Avenue between Jacob and Federal. There
is a sign in front of my house: KEYNES FUNERAL
PARLOR. I might have known. Instead of wounds,
bodies are dressed here. Where once the moist
coughs and soft groans of patients drifted up the
staircase, there is now the dry silence of the
newly dead. In the waiting room, no patients sit,
but corpses lie as once he lay in that very room
in a box lined with ruched satin. Is there no corner of this house to which a tenacious fragment
of her voice still clings? The topmost shelf of a
dark unused closet, perhaps, where, if I cocked
my ear, I might hear that last scrap of sound?

Listen! There she is at it again! Singing from
her polished walnut coffin. "The Blind Girl to
Her Harp," one of my favorites:

con expressivo

> In sorrow unto Thee I turn
> So touching is thy tone
> That list'ning to thy fitful woes
> Makes me forget my own.

No. No. All right. I imagined . . . a figment. Forget it. Only in his own kingdom has one the right
to go mad.

Suddenly, the street lamps go on. I go to
stand in the circle of light where Goldie had
looked up from her mirror. I bend to study the
sidewalk. Is that dark blotch? . . . No, the blood,
the scent of lily-of-the-valley, they too are all in
my mind.

I turn back toward the hotel. From an open

window the sound of a harmonica. Someone is playing "Santa Lucia." All at once, the whole gray, mythical, sad town quickens and begins to sway. I stop and move my hand in rhythm with the music. And a wave of happiness comes over me. I blink with amazement that the city of Troy still stands and that I, although gravid with my death, am here in it, and, like the pieces of Orpheus, sing on. Cassandra was right!

"Wheel round your horses, Greeks. Your conquest is ill-favored. Troy will live again."